ESSAYS
ON THE
CHURCH OF GOD

Essays
on the
Church of God

by
John Mitchell Mason

With a new introduction
by Guy Prentiss Waters

Presbyterian Press
Taylors, SC

© 2005

Presbyterian Press

Greenville Presbyterian Theological Seminary
P.O. Box 770
Taylors, SC 29687
www.gpts.edu
bookstore@gpts.edu

Printed in the United States of America

ISBN: 1-931639-08-6

Introduction to

John Mitchell Mason, *Essays on the Church of God*

It is my distinct pleasure to help welcome John M. Mason's *Essays on the Church of God* to a new generation of readers. Mason (1770-1829) was born in New York City to godly parents, his father a Scottish Presbyterian minister. Having graduated in 1789 from what is now Columbia University, he began theological studies under his father. He went to Scotland and continued his theological education under the direction of Drs. A. Hunter and John Erskine at the University of Edinburgh. His studies there were unexpectedly cut short by his father's death in 1792.

Mason immediately returned to the United States and began a profitable lifetime of service to the church. From 1793 to 1821 he served the Associate Reformed Church in New York City as pastor of two congregations. The first was his father's former charge, the Cedar Street Church, after which he moved to the Murray Street Church. In 1822, Mason transferred his credentials to the Presbyterian Church of the United States of America and assumed the presidency of Dickinson College in Pennsylvania. He served in this office until his failing health compelled him to resign in 1824.

Mason was a faithful churchman. He labored assiduously for the cause of foreign missions, and provided theological and pastoral leadership to the ARC during controversies surrounding the frequency of communion and the doctrine of justification by faith alone. One of the causes for which he exerted the greatest zeal and energy was an educated ministry. He drafted a plan, adopted by the ARC in 1808, for the institution and maintenance of congregational libraries. Owing in larger measure to Mason's leadership, the ARC in 1804 established a theological seminary according to a plan which he drafted. In addition to his pastoral responsibilities and amidst his travels to raise funds for the seminary's library, Mason served the seminary as its first and sole theological professor for over a decade. His ability as an educator was further acknowledged when Columbia named him Provost, a position he held from 1811 to 1816. Mason's sacrificial labors for the church were recognized in 1804 when the University of Pennsylvania awarded him the Doctor of Divinity (D.D.).

In 1806, Mason launched the influential "Christian's Magazine" to promote and defend confessional Presbyterianism. These *Essays on the*

Church of God were published serially in the "Christian's Magazine" between 1808 and 1810. A portion of them would be published separately in 1815. According to the editor of Mason's *Works* (1849), Mason left the *Essays* uncompleted. The absence of the discussion that Mason never included (the "mode of preserving a standing ministry") does not, however, compromise the integrity of the work.

Published in their entirety by the Presbyterian Board of Publication in 1843 and included within the two editions of his collected works (1832, 1849), Mason's *Essays* were studied by many nineteenth century Presbyterians. In 1844, the *Biblical Repertory and Princeton Review* reviewed them. They were assigned reading for Robert L. Dabney's students at Union Theological Seminary (Virginia). One need only peruse Thomas E. Peck's *Notes on Ecclesiology* (1892) to see Peck's liberal and favorable citations of Mason's *Essays*. Few Southern Presbyterian ministers educated at Union in the late nineteenth century would have been unacquainted with Mason's work.

Mason's work is of clear historical importance. What justifies reprinting it for the Presbyterian church of the twenty-first century? Let me suggest two reasons. First, Mason addresses questions of perennially practical importance to the church. On what terms or criteria should a session receive an adult individual into the membership of the church? (Essay 3) Are the infants of professing parents members of the visible church? And if so, why? (Essays 4-5) What is the church's obligation to the children of professing parents? What are those children's rights and duties? (Essay 7) Is the Christian ministry of divine warrant or of human origin? (Essay 8) What are the spiritual and intellectual qualifications for the Christian ministry? (Essays 9-10). Mason's discussions of these and other questions commend themselves to the modern reader for their clarity, penetration, and wisdom.

Mason's work is important for a second reason. It speaks to a number of issues that are troubling today's conservative Presbyterian church. We may cite two examples. Presbyterians have generally and rightly defended the doctrine of infant membership in the church. Some within the Reformed community, however, contend that we must speak of an undifferentiated church membership that warrants the admission of the children of believers to the Lord's Table. Readers will find in Mason's Essays a nuanced discussion of the nature and privileges of infant membership in the church that preserves the biblical and confessional distinction between non-communicant and communicant membership. Mason grounds his discussion of church membership in careful reflection on the nature of the church (Essay 1) and God's covenant with Abraham (Essay 2). Furthermore he is preeminently concerned to establish his case from the Scripture.

Another contemporary issue concerns sacramental efficacy, particularly the efficacy of baptism applied to children of the covenant. What does the sacrament of baptism *do*? In a day when troubling formulations of baptismal efficacy are in circulation within the Reformed church, we would do well to heed Mason's discussions in the fourth and sixth essays, especially the close of the latter. Here we find a positive and biblical exposition of baptism as a sacramental seal. This exposition is grounded in Mason's prior reflections on the biblical testimony concerning the covenant and the church.

In short, we have in Mason's *Essays* a biblical, confessional, and practical exposition of the doctrine of the church. Our Presbyterian fathers recognized in them much that is worthy of study and meditation. We would do well to follow in their footsteps. May the Lord be pleased to bless this work to the profit and edification of His church today.

Guy Prentiss Waters, Ph.D.
Assistant Professor of Biblical Studies
Belhaven College
Jackson, Mississippi

CONTENTS.

CHURCH OF GOD.

No. I.

It is our intention to lay before our readers in a series of numbers, a detailed but succinct account of the Church of God, embracing the chief questions concerning its nature, members, officers, order, worship, and the points directly connected with them. As we shall proceed upon a regular plan, the reader is requested not to form his judgment of the whole from an inspection of a part; and not to disjoin in his reflections those parts, which precede from those which follow; but to recur to the former as he meets with the latter, that the series of thought may be preserved unbroken in his mind; and that he may not accuse us hereafter with being superficial or negligent, when the blame ought possibly to be attached to his own memory. For having proved a point once, we shall not repeat the proof afterwards, unless for very particular reasons, and in a very summary way. We begin with

An inquiry into the meaning of the term CHURCH.

A community which has subsisted for ages, must always possess a number of usages and terms peculiar to itself. And although their origin may be remote, and their force unknown to many of its members, they suggest general ideas which serve the purposes of common conversation and common life. The fact may appear extraordinary, but it is nevertheless true; for the proportion of men in any society who analyze the words and phrases which they have been accustomed to utter ever since they were able to speak, is comparatively small. The reader can bring this matter to an easy test by interrogating himself concerning expressions which are coeval with his earliest recollection; and he will probably be surprised to find that, in thousands of instances, they have passed and repassed through his mind without his attempting to arrest them long enough to satisfy himself as to their appropriate sense. This want of precision is accompanied with no bad effect, till something occur to touch an institution, a privilege, or an observance, when the inconvenience may be sensibly felt. A popular notion is often overturned by the interpretation of a word; and the multitude are astonished either at their own mistake, or at the effrontery of those who charge them with committing it.

That which happens to all other durable combinations of men, must happen to the Christian Society. We need go no further for an example than its very name. "Church," "Christian Church," "Church of God," are familiar to the mouths of millions. They talk of "the Church" upon all occasions, without suspecting that perhaps they understand not what they say. They possibly never asked *what is the Church?* Possibly, they may think it too plain to deserve an answer. Possibly, also, the more they revolve it, the more they may be puzzled. Try the experiment. Put the question successively to several decent, intelligent men, and their replies, various as their previous religious habits, will convince you that their acquaintance with the subject is slight indeed. It is therefore necessary to go to first principles.

The word "Church," derived from the Greek κυριακὸν, signifies "the house of the Lord;" and marks the *property* which he has in it. But the original words which it is employed to translate, signify a different thing. The Hebrew words קהל (*cahal*) and עדה (*gheda*) in the Old Testament; and the corresponding one ἐκκλησια (*ecclesia*) in the New, all signify *an assembly*, especially one convened by invitation or appointment. That this is their generic sense, no scholar will deny; nor that their particular applications are ultimately resolvable into it. Hence it is evident, that from the terms themselves nothing can be concluded as to the nature or extent of the assembly which they denote. Whenever either of the two former occurs in the Old Testament, or the other in the New, you are sure of an *assembly*, but of nothing *more*. What that assembly is, and whom it comprehends, you must learn from the *connexion* of the term, and the *subject* of the writer. A few instances will exemplify the remark.

In the Old Testament קָהָל, (*cahal*) is applied

To the *whole mass* of the people, . *Ex.* xii. 6.

To a *portion* of the people, who came upon Hezekiah's invitation to keep the passover.

2 Chron. xxx. 24.

To the *army* of Pharaoh. . . *Ezek.* xvii. 17.

To an *indefinite multitude*. . . *Gen.* xxviii. 3.

To the society of Simeon and Levi.   xlix. 6.

So also עֵדָה, (*gheda*) is applied

To the *whole* nation of Israel. *Ex.* xvi. 22;

xxxv. 1.

To the *particular* company of Korah, Dathan, and Abiram. . . . . *Numb.* xvi. 16.

To the assembly of the *just*, as opposed to the *wicked*. . . . . *Psal.* i. 5.

To the *judicatory*, before which crimes were tried. . . . . . . *Numb.* xxxv. 12. 24; compared with *Deut.* xix. 12. 17. 18.

In like manner ἐκκλησία, (*ecclesia*) rendered "Church," is applied

To the *whole body* of the redeemed.

Ephes. v. 24. 27.

To the *whole body* of professing Christians.

1 *Cor.* xii. 28.

To *local* organizations of professing Christians, whether more or less extensive ; as in the apostolic salutations, and inscriptions of the epistles.

To a *small association* of Christians meeting together in a private house. *Col.* iv. 15.—*Phil.* i. 2.

To a civil assembly *lawfully* convened.

Act. xix. 39.

To a body of people *irregularly* convened.

Act. xix. 32.

This specimen is sufficient to show that no person can answer the question, " what is the *Church?*" without carefully examining the *thing* as well as the *name :* nor safely expound either, without consulting the original scriptures ; or putting himself implicitly under the direction of one who is able to do it for him. An attempt to discuss the constitution and order of the church, without looking much further and much deeper than the mere *term*, as it occurs in our English Bibles, can never be any better than childish prattle.

I have said that the term " Church" is applied to the whole body of professing Christians ; and my design is to prove that the scriptures teach the doctrine of *a Visible Church Catholic*, composed of all those throughout the world who profess the true religion.

This great society is a " Church," because it is

collected together by the authority of God in the dispensation of the gospel, and solemnly set apart from the world for sacred uses.

This church is " visible," as distinguished from the " elect of God," who are known to him alone ; and therefore cannot, *as such*, form a separate society among men.

This visible church is " Catholic," that is, it comprehends all those " throughout the world that profess the true religion."

If then I am asked what I mean by the " Church?" I answer, that visible catholic society which I have now defined ; which is the kingdom of our Lord Jesus Christ upon earth, where he has deposited his truth, and instituted his ordinances.

The fact that he has founded such a church, I thus demonstrate.

1. It is indisputable that such a church did formerly exist, and that by his own appointment.

The whole of the covenanted seed of Abraham belonged to it. That this " seed" made up the church of God under the law ; that it embraced, at least in some periods, thousands and ten thousands within and without the land of Judea, and among them multitudes who never were partakers of saving grace, cannot be doubted. Every one who had the token of God's covenant in his flesh, whether regenerated or not, was reputed a member of this church. The Jews were scattered, by several dispersions, through distant lands ; yet preserving the name of the God of their fathers, and their profession of adherence to him, they were never considered as cast out of his church. On this ground it was, that on the day of pentecost, " there were dwelling at Jerusalem, Jews, devout men, out of *every nation under heaven.*"* The old economy was subjected to local restrictions which rendered a universal dispensation impossible while they lasted, but still the " professors of the true religion," the worshippers of the God of Israel, made up but *one* church. Reside where they might, they all belonged to the יהוה‎ קהל‎, the congregation of the Lord.

If, then, there is no longer any public church visible, what has become of it ? Who has annulled, destroyed, blotted it out ? Produce a single declaration of its divine author that it should come to an end. The disinheriting of the unhappy Jews is nothing to the purpose, or rather supports the contrary. Their being cast out of the visible church, for they could not be cast out of any other, implies the existence of that church, and the privilege of connexion with her. The abolition of those restrictions which were suited to a preparatory state, fitted her for universality. But that which fitted her for universality could in no sense whatever be her annihilation. The Jews

* Act. ii. 5.

were not cut off, till after the commencement and establishment of the new dispensation, that is, till after the Gentiles were taken in: therefore the visible church, as an organized whole, subsisted after the commencement of this dispensation, and that among the Gentile Christians. And the excision of the Jews was no more an extermination of the visible church, than the lopping off a diseased branch is felling the whole tree. It is incumbent on them who deny a visible catholic church under the New Testament, to show at what time, by what authority, and by what means, so signal a constitution of God has been laid aside.

2. The Old Testament scriptures proceed on the principle that the visible church state, co-extensive with the Redeemer's kingdom upon earth, was *not* to cease at the introduction of the evangelical dispensation.

There are numerous predictions concerning the church, and numerous promises to her, in her *public* capacity, which are unfulfilled at this hour, and never can be fulfilled, if her visible unity be not asserted. For example: " Esaias saith, there shall be a root of Jesse, and he that shall rise to reign over the Gentiles: in him shall the Gentiles trust." Does any man suppose that the " reign" of the Redeemer " over the Gentiles" is confined to those whom his grace has subdued to the " obedience of faith ?" And if not, that his kingdom, destitute of a distinctive mark, is broken down into detached fragments, resembling not a compact community, but a hord of petty democracies? The very idea of a kingdom proves that his church is one, that she is visible, and that this visible unity is one of her essential attributes. If you cut her up into ten thousand pieces, there is no more a kingdom. If you strip her of visible form, you contract her within limits of which Omniscience alone is the judge; you withdraw her from the eyes of men altogether; and shut her up in impenetrable secrecy. Where then is her light? Where her testimony? Where the use of those cautions, precepts, encouragements, which are adapted to her state as *visible*, and have no meaning in any other application?

Thus, " I will extend peace to her like a river, and the glory of the Gentiles like a flowing stream."*—" Kings shall be thy nursing-fathers, and their queens thy nursing-mothers."† " The Gentiles shall come to thy light, and kings to the brightness of thy rising—the abundance of the, sea shall be converted into thee; the forces of the Gentiles shall come unto thee."‡—These are but a very small sample of prophecies which run in the same general strain: and two things are obvious on the bare inspection of them.

First, that they contemplate the church as *one* :

* Is. lxvi. 12.   † Is. xlix. 23.   ‡ Is. lx. 3. 5.

for she is introduced as a single person; and under this idea are they addressed to her.

Second—That this unity is not ascribed to her as composed of the elect alone. The Gentiles who should flow into her were not all, nor are pretended to have been, real Christians: that "light" which was to shine upon the Gentiles, and the "brightness" of that "rising" which was to attract the "kings," must of necessity be *external*: nor could kings be her "nursing-fathers," nor their queens her "nursing-mothers," but as a public society which they could *distinguish*. In any other sense the prediction is palpably false.

Further: when he foretells the transition of the dispensation of grace from the Jews to the Gentiles, the prophet uses the same style. He represents the church not as subsisting in a vast multitude of independent associations, but as a great *whole ;* as possessing individual unity. He personifies it, as in the former instances : " Sing, O barren, that thou didst not bear : break forth into singing, and cry aloud, that thou didst not travail with child ; for more are the children of the desolate, than the children of the married wife, saith the Lord. Enlarge the place of thy tent, and let them stretch forth the curtains of thy habitations ; spare not ; lengthen thy cords, and strengthen thy stakes."*

Is. xliv. 1. 2.

This is, unequivocally, a description of the church as exhibited under an outward dispensation. The comparison between the " desolate" and the " married wife," can have no place in a question concerning the *internal* church, nor do the other circumstances at all agree to her.

Indeed, whoever admits that there was, at any time past, *one* visible church, and that promises were made to her, of which some have had, others are receiving, and others are yet to have, their accomplishment, must of course admit the continuance of that church at present. For the *fulfilling* a promise *to* an individual or a society, supposes the existence of that individual or society. The promises, for example, to Israel, could never have been performed, had Israel perished. The adoption of another family might have been accompanied with other promises, or with the renewal of the old ones : but, in no sense could they be *fulfilled* to a race which was extinct before the time of fulfilment came. The fact, then, that God is *now* fulfilling, and to fulfil *hereafter*, promises given to the visible church ages ago, establishes her perpetuity and identity. She never has been destroyed, or she could not at *this day* enjoy the accomplishment of *ancient* promise

3. The language of the New Testament implies, that an external visible church state *was* not abo lished with the law of Moses.

The writers of the New Testament never go about to *prove* that there is a catholic visible church; far less do they speak of it as *originating* in the evangelical dispensation; but they assume its existence, as a point which no Christian in their days ever thought of disputing. They argue against schism, upon the principle that the visible church is one, and they record ecclesiastical deliberations, and decisions by the apostles and elders, which, upon any other principle, were downright usurpation of dominion over conscience. This last particular, will be more fully handled before we have done. Let us, in the mean time, attend to some instances in which this doctrine of the one visible church, is interwoven with the texture of their language.

" This is he that was with the *church* in the wilderness." Acts vii. 38. Stephen refers to Moses, and we know what church Moses was with. No one, in his right mind, will undertake to say that Moses was with the elect only. " Our fathers," adds the martyr, " would not obey him." Moses himself writes that these rebels were the " people"—the " whole congregation"—" all the children of Israel,"* and this was the " church" to which Stephen refers.

" The Lord added to the *church* daily such as should be saved." Acts ii. 47. " Saul made

* Ex. xxxii. Num. xiv.

havoc of the *church.*" Ch. viii. 3.—" God hath set some in the *church ;* first, apostles," &c. 1 Cor. xii. 28.—" Gaius, the host of the whole *church.*" Rom. xvi. 23.—" Give none offence to the *church of God.*" 1 Cor. x. 32.—" I persecuted the *church of God.*" 1 Cor. xv. 9.

The list might easily be swelled ; but it is needless. Let us weigh the import of these passages. The " church," to which the Lord daily added such as should be saved, was not the body of the elect, for no addition can be made to them ; nor was it a single congregation, unless God had no more people to be saved in Jerusalem, than, together with mere professors, were sufficient for one pastoral charge. Nor is it to be imagined either that Saul confined his persecution to one congregation ; or that he was able to pick out the elect, and persecute them. As little can it be suspected, either that Gaius never entertained any but the elect, or that his entertainments never went beyond one congregation. Nor will a sober man allege, that God hath set no officers but in one congregation, or that they have no functions toward any but his elect ; or that all whom he hath set are themselves of the number ; nor yet, that " offence" can never be given to any but to the elect. The sin, to be committed at all, requires both that the offending and offended, may see and know each other. But the scripture is

express: The Lord added to the *church*—Saul
persecuted the *church*—Gaius was the host of the
church—God hath set officers in the *church*—
Christians are not to offend the *church*. Now as
these and many similar phrases, are utterly inap-
plicable either to a single congregation, or to the
body of the redeemed, they must designate another
and different society, which can be no other than
what we have called the visible Church Catholic.
Too extensive for partial assemblies, too notorious for any secret election of men, and yet a
church; *the* church—it is *general, external,* and
but ONE.

In truth, the phraseology of the New Testament
on this subject, as on many others, is borrowed
directly from that of the Old. The expression
" church of God," is a literal translation into English of those Greek words which are themselves
a literal translation from the Hebrew. For every
scholar knows, that קְהַל הָאֱלֹהִים or קְהַל יְהוָה; ἐκκλησία
θεοῦ; and " Church of God," signify in their respective tongues, exactly the same thing. Conceive, then, of an apostle's addressing himself to
Jews, as Paul did, in the Hebrew tongue. By
what phrase would he designate the church?
Evidently by that which is used in the Hebrew
scriptures, and was familiar to his hearers. And
what sense could they put upon it? Evidently that
which had long been settled, and no other. Would

the Jews, then, have understood him as meaning by "the church," either a section of their nation no bigger than could be contained within the walls of a synagogue? or those favoured ones whom God has predestined to life? The thing is impossible! because he would use the current phraseology of both their holy and their popular language in a sense quite different from any which had formerly been affixed to it. They would understand him as discoursing of that great visible society which God had publicly set apart for himself.

Conceive again of the apostle as addressing Gentiles on this subject, and speaking Greek. He would evidently express himself in the terms which he *has* used in his epistles. What ἐκκλησία (*ecclesia*) means, every Grecian could tell. But how was a Heathen to understand the meaning of ἐκκλησία θεοῦ (*ecclesia theou*,) or the "church of God?" He was perfectly ignorant of Christian doctrine, and the structure of Christian congregations. Nor could he form any correct notion of the thing intended, without an explanation drawn from the Old Testament scriptures.

The result stands thus: The apostle, when preaching or writing to Jews or Gentiles, speaks of the church of God in terms well known to the one, and entirely new to the other. The alternative is obvious. Either he used these terms in their ascertained sense, or not. If the former, he has recognized the visible unity of the Church Catholic; and so our position is proved. If the latter, he deceived all his hearers; all his correspondents; all who in every age adopt his letters as a rule of faith. Undoubtedly, had he used the terms " church" and " church of God" in a sense unknown to Moses and the Fathers, he would not have omitted to mention it; that we might not be led into errour. But the fact is, that there is not throughout the New Testament any exposition of these terms. They are employed as terms of the most definite import; as terms which no one who chose to consult the earlier scriptures could mistake. The law of interpretation to the primitive Christians must, of course, be our law; and the same issue returns upon us; the expression " church of God," used without qualification, means an external society comprehending all those who profess the true religion.

If any one think that too much stress is laid upon the coincidence between the phraseology of the two Testaments, let him reflect, not only that they relate to a common whole; but that the same coincidence happens in other things. Thus, " Christ," is but the English form of Χριστος, which is the literal translation of משׁיח, (Messiah) all signifying " the anointed." When, therefore, the Lord Jesus was proclaimed as the " Christ of

God," how could either Jew or Gentile understand the preacher but by going back to the Old Testament? There the word was perfectly familiar, although, in its sacred sense, utterly unknown to the Heathen. And this explains why a profession that " Jesus is the Christ," was deemed, in the first age of the church, a sufficient criterion of one's religion. No man could make it without being instructed, from the scriptures of the Old Testament, in the Redeemer's character and work. The reason why many now suppose such a profession extremely easy, is, that they do not perceive its relation to truths previously revealed. And this, too, is the reason why there is so much blundering about the nature of the church. People imagine themselves at liberty to interpret the word at their pleasure : whereas it is referrible to the Old Testament as really as the word "Christ." Neither the nature of the church, nor the office of her head, is to be understood without an appeal to the same scriptures. Consequently, that very rule which expounds " the Christ of God," as signifying one who was qualified by the father's appointment, and by the measureless communication of the divine Spirit, to be a Saviour for men; will oblige us to expound the " church of God," as signifying that great visible society which professes his name.

4. The account which the New Testament

gives of the church, confirms the doctrine of her visible unity.

One of the most common appellations by which she is there distinguished, is, " the kingdom of heaven." This can be but one: or else it would not be *a* kingdom, and *the* kingdom, but several. And this one must be visible, because its ordinances are administered by visible agency.* Nay it is only *as visible* that it admits of the exercise of any part of its government by men. The church invisible, which eludes every human sense and faculty, cannot be the object of human functions. And to preclude mistake in this matter, our Lord informs us that his kingdom, while in the world, shall, like other kingdoms, have false as well as true subjects. That hypocrites shall so intermingle with saints as to render their separation in the present life impossible by any means which will not exterminate both. Such is the manifest import of the parable of the " tares." Mat. xiii. 24—30.

An attempt has, indeed, been made, to repel this argument, by supposing the parable to represent, not the mixture of Christians with hypocrites in *the church*, but their mixture with wicked men in *civil Society.* Let us see:

The parable is a likeness of " the kingdom of heaven." A phrase which never signifies the

* Mat. xvi. 19. xxviii. 19, 20. John xx. 21—23.

world at large, or civil society; but the church of
God under the evangelical dispensation. There
was no need to teach the disciples, by a symboli-
cal lesson, that good men and bad are mingled together in civil society. This had been sufficiently
attested by the experience of all previous ages,
and was at that very moment evident to their
eyes. But considering the expectations which
they might be led to form from the introduction
of a spiritual economy, it was altogether needful
to apprise them that in her best estate, in her
noblest appearance as the kingdom of Heaven,
the church would be still imperfect, and injured
by unworthy members. Nor could the officers of
Christ, answering to the " servants of the house-
holder," ever entertain so wild an idea as that of
severing Christians from the society of other men;
for were it even practicable, it would defeat one
of the high ends for which they live in the world;
that of " letting their light shine before others;"
and would gradually extirpate them from the
face of the earth. But it would be very natural
for the disciples to imagine that, with the keys of
the kingdom of Heaven in their hands, they
should endeavour to exclude every one whom
they had reason to suspect of insincerity. Many
are infected with such a notion to this day. No
rotten hearted professor shall pollute their communion ! they will rest the right of admission

upon the *reality* of conversion! And some waste
their lives in pursuit of that chimera, a perfect
church! Nór have either the admonitions of
Christ, nor the rough tuition of disappointment,
cured them of their folly. There was, therefore,
much cause for guarding his disciples against so
imposing an errour. And he has taught them
that there are no human means of effecting a
complete expulsion of the unconverted from his
church: that the attempt would destroy his own
people: and, therefore, that they must be left,
like the tares and the wheat, to " grow together
until the harvest." Then, that is, at " the end
of the world," he will " send forth his angels,
and they shall gather out of"—what ? Civil
society ? No, but out of " *his kingdom*, all things
that offend ; and them which do iniquity, and
shall cast them into a furnace of fire : there shall
be weeping and gnashing of teeth."—v. 41, 42.

To the same amount is the parable of the net,
in verses 47—50. " The kingdom of heaven is
like unto a net that was cast into the sea, and
gathered of every kind." Is this, too, a description of civil society ? It is evident, that " the sea,"
with its swarms of fishes, represents the world
with its multitudes of men. Like a net cast into
the former, the kingdom of heaven introduced
among the latter, gathers a mixed assemblage
from the common mass. And as it is impossible,

while the net is in the waters, to divide the good
fish from the bad; so it is impossible, while the
kingdom of heaven exists here among men,
to divide saints from hypocrites. The alternative is alike in the type, and the thing typified.
The net must be drawn " to shore," before the
fish can be distributed; the kingdom of heaven
must close; " the end of the world" must come,
before " the wicked can be severed from among
the just." Nothing can be clearer, than that mankind at large correspond, in the parable, with the
fish of the sea; consequently, that the kingdom of
heaven, which, like a net thrown into the sea,
gathers a *selection* from among men, cannot possibly mean civil society. To make this out, it
should be proved that the net catches *all* the fish
wherever it is cast into the sea.

To crown this argument; the kingdom of heaven is likened unto " ten virgins, of whom five
were wise, and five were foolish."* This also
must mean " civil society," or the hypothesis we
are considering is ruined. But what man in his
senses will venture upon so extravagant an assertion? *All* these virgins professed to belong to the
train of the bridegroom—*All* the members of civil
society make no such profession. It is wasting
words to press the point further. This notion of
the state of civil society being represented by the

* Mat. xxv. 1.

parable of the tares, &c. is a fable invented in order to get rid of a troublesome truth : and adds
another to the numberless examples already given
by zeal without knowledge, of its being much
easier to contradict the scriptures, than to explain
them. The sum is,

That the kingdom of heaven cannot designate
the election of grace; because no one belonging
to that will be " cast into the furnace of fire."—
We have proved that it cannot signify the state of
civil society, and it would be superlatively ridiculous to confine it to a single congregation; therefore,

It must mean the *external Visible Church,* which,
according to the conditions of description, can be
but ONE.

If we proceed a little further, we shall meet
with the same thing under a different form. The
apostle Paul, in his first letter to the Corinthian
Christians, chap. xii. treats at length, of the various gifts which the Holy Spirit had bestowed
upon various individuals. He argues that these
gifts ought to be no ground of dissention, for these
two reasons : *first,* that they were all of the same
divine original ; and *secondly,* that they all contributed to the common good, and most effectually
by retaining each its appropriate place. The
latter reason is illustrated by the analogy of the
human body; and winds up with declaring—

" Now ye are the body of Christ, and members in particular." The question is, what are we to understand by the " body of Christ ?"

That it signifies a *whole*, is as plain as that words signify any thing. Then, *what* whole? Not the church at Corinth, far less a particular congregation, unless the commission of the apostles and the use of all spiritual gifts, extend no further.

Not the church of the elect; for there are no " schisms" in that body, as *such*. A schism which cannot be perceived is no schism; and the moment you render it perceptible, you are in a visible church. Nor can it be affirmed, but at the expense of all fact and consistency, that God hath set no officers except in the church of his redeemed. For, upon that supposition, no church officer could ever exercise his office toward any non-elected man; the pastoral relation could never be fixed without knowing beforehand who are the elected of God; or else, no person, however blasphemous and abominable, could be kept out of a church, because such " blasphemer and injurious" may possibly be " a chosen vessel." These are absurdities.

But a body, a church there is, in which " God hath set, first, apostles; secondarily, prophets; thirdly, teachers," &c. An individual congregation it is not. A partial coalescence of congre-

gations it is not.   The " church of the first-born
whose names are written in heaven," it is not :
and yet it is a church ; *the* church to which God
hath given his ordinances.   There is no escape ;
it can be no other than what we have called the
Visible Church Catholic.

The reader has been more inattentive than it
would be fair to suspect of any who shall peruse
these sheets, if he has not remarked, that all the
means of salvation are external.   The scriptures,
the sabbath, the solemn assembly, the sacraments,
the ministry ; in a word, the whole system of instituted worship, is visible.   Now, is it not a most
incredible thing, that the church and the ordinances committed to her, should be of opposite
natures ?   Or rather, that the ordinances should
have a solid, external existence, and the church
to which they are given, no such existence at all !
A visible bible, visible ministry, visible worship,
visible sacraments, visible discipline, and no visible church ! Nothing but a phantom, a metaphysi-
cal idea, as the repository of God's truth and
institutions ! One fact in the history of revelation,
is enough to dispel these visions.   It will not be
controverted that the scriptures are God's testimony to his church.   But more than one half of
this testimony was delivered to the Israelites in
their public covenanted character ; for " unto
them were committed the oracles of God."   Unto

whom, then, have the subsequent scriptures been committed? "Unto the New Testament Church," you will say. Agreed. But the question falls back upon you, what is the New Testament Church? If she is not the very same great society which God formerly erected for the praise of his glory, and has caused to pass under a new form of dispensation, three consequences follow :

1st, That the Old Testament is no part of the trust deposited with her, and belongs not to the rule of her faith.

2d. That God has divided his testimony between two churches of the most different nature; and of which one has long been extinct. Therefore,

3d. That the whole scriptures, as the testimony of God, never were, nor can be, committed to any church whatever, unless in virtue of another special revelation.

But if, on the contrary, these scriptures are the testimony of God deposited with his church, then it irresistibly follows, that she is now, and ever has been, since her first organization, a public visible society which God has appropriated to himself; where his name is known, and his mercies are vouchsafed.

And, indeed, the general principle of the church visible is so inseparable from the Christian style and doctrine, that its most strenuous opposers are unconsciously admitting it every hour of their

lives.   They talk habitually of " the church; the
faith of the church; the worship of the church;
the sufferings of the church; God's dealings
with his church," and a thousand things of like
import.   Let them ask what they mean by such
expressions ?   They will not say, " a particular
congregation ;" and if they say " the election of
grace," they will speedily contradict themselves,
and fact, and the word of God too.   Their whole
language, as Christians, is accommodated to the
very thing, which, in form, they renounce.   There
is no getting along without it.   No ingenuity can
enable them to converse five minutes together
about the church of God, as existing on earth,
without the introduction of an idea different from
either of those which they affix to that term :
and this third idea, if they will be at the trouble to
analyze it, will turn out to be no other than that of
the *Visible Church Catholic.*

We have now developed our views of that
phrase, " the church," and assigned our reasons
for them : the reader will, therefore, recollect,
when he meets with it in the course of our disquisitions, that we mean by it the aggregate body
of those who profess the true religion: all making
up but ONE Society, of which the Bible is the statute book; Jesus Christ the head; and a covenant relation the uniting bond.

CHURCH OF GOD.

No. II.

On its first Organization.

In the preceding number we have proved the
existence of a *Visible Church Catholic ;* and that
this is the thing intended by such spiritual phrases
as " the Church of God," " the house of God,"
" the kingdom of heaven." But it does not more
certainly exist, than it exists in virtue of a divine
interposition. None but the living God could set
up, protect, and govern, his own kingdom. The
question is, when, and where, and how, so singular a society was instituted ? The question is of
moment, as being connected with interesting
views of the external economy of salvation. Let
us attempt to answer it.

We know by experience that the church of
God was in the world before us. So did our fathers. So did the previous generation : and in
this manner the historical fact may be deduced
from the days of the apostles. The " Church,"

therefore, has not been created since their days. Was it created then ? No : the apostles found it, as we found it, older than themselves. Their writings are full of its privileges, its ordinances, and other peculiarities ; but contain not a single hint of its *originating* with them. They uniformly *suppose* its prior establishment, and speak of it as having been long and familiarly understood. Guided by the clue which they have put into our hands, we go back to the books of the prophets, and meet the same supposition there. We proceed, with similar success, through the Levitical law, and the Sinai-covenant ; we pass the age of Moses, and arrive at the *Father of the faithful.* Here the clue runs out. No ingenuity can follow it further. People of God there were ; promises of God there were ; gracious revelations, and acceptable worship of God, there were : but a *Church of God,* organized upon the principle of *visible unity,* and standing in such relation to him as it did in after ages ; such a Church, before the vocation of Abram, there was not, nor any thing which bore the semblance of it. For its original organization ; for the germ of that great system into which it has already grown, and shall yet grow, we must look among the transactions of that memorable period which elapsed between the call of Abram in Ur of the Chaldees, and the birth of his son Isaac.

On the first of these occasions Jehovah gave him a double promise :

1. A promise of a numerous progeny, and great personal prosperity. *I will make of thee a great nation ; and I will bless thee, and make thy name great, and thou shalt be a blessing ; and I will bless them that bless thee, and curse him that curseth thee.—Gen.* xii. 2, 3.

2. The promise of his being a medium of conveying extensive blessings to the world. *In thee shall all families of the earth be blessed.*—v. 3.

All the subsequent communications which God made to him are referrible to one of these two promises. They were both called up at different intervals, explained, expanded, and confirmed, till each of them became the basis of an appropriate *covenant.* Let us briefly mark their progress.

1. The promise of a numerous progeny is repeated with an engagement to bestow upon them the land of Canaan, ch. xii. 7. This promise was stated and confirmed in the most precise and ample terms, after Abram had separated from Lot, ch. xiii. 14. 17. And finally, as he was advancing in years, and the probability of its accomplishment was proportionably diminishing, the Lord " came to him in a vision," and having cheered him with this gracious assurance, *I am thy shield, and thy exceeding great reward,* ch. xv. 1,

renewed the promise concerning his seed, as that which should come forth out of his own bowels and be multiplied as the stars of heaven. The patriarch on this occasion so glorified the divine veracity by his unshaken, unquestioning faith, that the scripture saith, *it was counted to him for righteousness*, verse 6. The renewed promise concerning his progeny was immediately followed by a confirmation of the grant of Canaan; and a remarkable pledge that the grant should be executed in due season. Having, as he had been commanded, slain several animals, divided their bodies, and placed the sections opposite to each other, his senses were locked up to every other object, and Jehovah disclosed to him a comprehensive view of evils to come upon his family before their possession of the promised land. But their possession at the proper time was guaranteed by solemn compact. "A burning lamp," the symbol of the divine presence, " passed between those pieces" of the slain animals, in token of ratifying every stipulation belonging to the promise in question. For *in that same day, the Lord made a* COVENANT *with Abram, saying,* " *Unto thy seed have I given this land,*" &c. v. 8—21.

Here is an end of all transactions for establishing the first promise. It was sealed in the *covenant*, and never again occurs by itself The end of this covenant, too well defined to be mistaken, was to secure to Abram a numerous posterity, and their inheritance in the land of Canaan. Further it went not. It does not so much as mention the promise relating to the families of the earth being blessed in him. And from the minuteness with which every thing else is adjusted, it is evident that this last promise, not even hinted at, was not intended to be comprised in the covenant which secured the other. Let us proceed then.

2. Fourteen years after the date of this covenant, Jehovah appeared again to Abram, and made another covenant with him. The transaction is thus recorded in the seventeenth chapter of Genesis: *And when Abram was ninety years old and nine, the* LORD *appeared to Abram, and said unto him, I* am *the Almighty God; walk before me, and be thou perfect. And I will make my covenant between me and thee; and will multiply thee exceedingly. And Abram fell on his face: and God talked with him, saying, As for me, behold my covenant is with thee, and thou shalt be a* FATHER OF MANY NATIONS. *Neither shall thy name any more be called Abram; but thy name shall be* Abraham: *for a father of many nations have I made thee. And I will make thee exceeding fruitful, and I will make nations of thee; and kings shall come out of thee. And I will establish my covenant between me and thee, and thy seed after thee, in their generations,*

for an everlasting covenant ; to be A GOD UNTO THEE,
AND TO THY SEED AFTER THEE. *And I will give unto
thee, and to thy seed after thee, the land wherein thou
art a stranger, all the land of Canaan, for an everlasting possession ; and I will be their God. And God
said unto Abraham, Thou shalt keep my covenant
therefore, thou, and thy seed after thee, in their generations. This is my covenant which ye shall keep between me and you, and thy seed after thee ; Every
man-child among you shall be* CIRCUMCISED. *And ye
shall circumcise the flesh of your foreskin ; and it shall
be a token of the covenant betwixt me and you. And
he that is eight days old shall be circumcised among
you, every man-child in your generations ; he that is
born in the house, or bought with money of any
stranger, which* IS NOT OF THY SEED. *He that is born
in thy house and he that is bought with thy money,
must needs be circumcised : and my covenant shall be
in your flesh for an everlasting covenant. And the
uncircumcised man-child, whose flesh of his foreskin
is not circumcised, that soul shall be cut off from his
people ; he hath broken my covenant, ver.* 1—14.

Our inquiry is into the nature and design of
this covenant. What was it ?

Not a covenant, either of works or grace, for
eternal life. For Abram had been " justified
by faith, without the works of the law," and had
been interested in the covenant of God's grace

before this. His eternal life had been secured many years.

Nor was it merely a personal or domestic covenant: that is, one which provided for the individual dignity of the patriarch, and the prosperous settlement of his children in the land of Canaan. This, too, had been concluded long before, as has been shown. It recognizes, indeed, all that was included in the personal covenant, which it might otherwise be supposed to supersede; but it has features of its own so peculiar and marked, that it cannot be considered in any other light than that of a distinct engagement.

For, besides the solemnity with which it was introduced, and which would hardly have preceded a mere repetition of former grants, it contained new matter; it constituted new relations; and was affirmed in an extraordinary manner.

1st. It contained new *matter*—*I will make thee a father of many nations:* which is much more than can be interpreted of Abram's literal posterity; and must be viewed as expounding the promise and extending the privilege formerly assured to him—*In thee shall all families of the earth be blessed.* It was a great thing to be only an instrument of blessing to all the families of the earth; but a much greater to be that instrument in such a manner as to become what no other man, in the sense of the covenant, ever did, or ever can be-

come, "a *father* of many nations:" and moreover, a personal pledge, also, of his new dignity
was conferred upon the patriarch, in that remarkable alteration of his name from Abram to Abraham; the former signifying *high Father;* and the
latter, *high Father of a multitude.*

2d. It constituted new relations—*To be a God
unto thee, and to thy seed after thee.* This cannot
be explained of Abraham's relation to God as the
God of his salvation; for in that sense God was
his God long before; and whatever is the relation expressed, it grew out of the covenant *now
made;* It embraced his *seed* too. Nor, with respect to *their* eternal life, did God now engage to
be their God; for all that was adjusted in the covenant of grace ; and the privilege could not reach
beyond those who were the actual partakers of
the same precious faith with Abraham. Whereas, in the sense of *this* covenant, God was the God
of all Abraham's seed, without exception, under the
limitations which restricted the covenant operation first to Isaac, and afterwards to Jacob, inclu-
ding such as should choose their God, their faith,
and their society. For he was to be their God in
their generations : i. e. as soon as a new individual
of this seed was generated, he was within the
covenant; and according to the tenour of the
covenant, God was his God.*

* The expressions "thy God," "my God," "our God," and
that, so much and so properly in use among Christians, "our

The foregoing retrospect has decided one point, to wit, that *the covenant with Abraham and his seed, contemplated them not primarily nor immediately, as of the election of grace, but as an aggregate which it severed from the bulk of mankind; and placed in a social character under peculiar relations to the most high God.* To define precisely the nature of this constitution, we must go a step further, and ascertain who are meant by "the seed."

It cannot be the carnal descendants of Abraham exclusively; although it has a particular respect to them, for,

(1.) Three large branches of that seed were actually shut out of the covenant, i. e. the children of Ishmael, of Esau, and of Keturah.

covenant God," must always be interpreted according to the nature of the covenant to which they refer. Common, but unwarranted practice, has limited them to the covenant of grace; so that a serious man is apt to think he hears heresy, if they be ever applied to any thing else than the saving relation in which a believer stands to God as his reconciled God in Christ Jesus. But this is a mistake; and lies at the foundation of many false and hurtful opinions of the Christian Church and its privileges. The Jews could, *nationally*, call God "their God:" They often did so, and with right, when they were gross hypocrites in the article of their personal religion. The Sinai-covenant constituted them the people of Jehovah, and him their God, as really, but in a widely different sense, as he was the covenant God of Abraham, or of Paul, for personal salvation. A due exposition of this matter involves the whole doctrine of the visible church catholic, which is grievously misunderstood by most professing Christians of all denominations.

(2.) The covenant provided for the admission of others, who never belonged to that seed. *He that is eight days old shall be circumcised among you ; every man-child in your generations : he that is born in the house or bought with money of any stranger, which is* NOT OF THY SEED.

This principle was acted upon under the constitution which was superadded, by the ministry of Moses, 430 years after. The stranger who wished to keep the passover, was required first to circumcise all his males, and then he became as *one born in the land,* i. e. he was to all intents and purposes under the full operation of the covenant established with Abraham and his seed. On the other hand, the Edomite, *who sprung from the loins of Abraham,* was put upon the *same footing* with the Egyptian who descended from Ham: the children of both were received in the fourth generation; neither of them came in upon the plea of consanguinity with Abraham: nor were they admitted into the commonwealth of Israel under the idea of the children of Israel having Abraham for their literal father, but formally and explicitly upon the ground of their being " *the congregation of the Lord.*" Deut. xxiii. 8.* But, being once incor-

---

* קהל יהוה " The church of Jehovah :" the very expression which is translated again and again in the New Testament, εκκλησια θεου, " the church of God." The fact is, that all our lan guage in sacred things is borrowed from the Old Testament ; and

porated with the natural seed, in that great congregation, they, too, were viewed as of the covenanted seed; and they transmitted their privilege to their children in their generations.

(3.) By the covenant made with Abraham he acquired the prerogative of being the "*father of many nations.*" This article is, of itself, a demonstration that the covenant was of a much wider extent than all the literal descendants of Abraham in the line of Jacob put together. They never did make but *one* nation. There is a marked distinction between them and these " many nations ;" who are evidently the same with "all the families of the earth," that were to be blessed in Abraham. The apostle Paul interprets the phrase by another; his being "the *heir of the world;*" and peremptorily denies its restriction to the literal seed. *Rom.* iv. 13, 16, 17.

The argument is short. Abraham's seed comprehends all those to whom he is the father: but he is the father of many nations; therefore, these many nations are to be accounted as his seed. Again: the covenant was made with Abraham and with his seed: therefore, the covenant embra-

cannot be understood without a reference to it; and those who clamourously demand the origin of every thing Christian to be produced from the New Testament, show that they understand neither the New Testament nor the Old, nor yet that very Christianity about which they prate. Christianity is more, a great deal more, than a few doctrines.

ced these many nations who are included in his
seed.

3. This covenant was affirmed in an extraordinary manner; *viz.* by the rite of *circumcision.*
This, saith God, *is my covenant which ye shall keep
between me and you, and thy . seed after thee, every
man-child among you shall be circumcised.*   The
uses of this rite were two.

First. It certified to the seed of Abraham, by a
token in the flesh of their males, that the covenant
· with their great progenitor was in force; that they
were under its full operation; and entitled to all
the benefits immediately derived from it.   But
circumcision had a further use; for,

Secondly, The apostle Paul informs us that it
was *a seal of the* RIGHTEOUSNESS OF THE FAITH *which*
Abraham *had, being yet uncircumcised, that he might
be the father of all them that believe, though they be not
circumcised ; that* RIGHTEOUSNESS MIGHT BE IMPUTED
unto them also.   Rom. iv. 11.   In this connexion
it certified,

That Abraham was justified by *faith* .

That the doctrine and the privilege of the
" righteousness of faith," were to be perpetuated
among his seed by the operation of God's covenant with him :

That the justification of a sinner is by faith
alone; " righteousness" being " imputed" to all
them that *believe,*" and to them only ; who by the

very fact of their *believing*, become, in the highest sense, children of Abraham, and are accordingly blessed with him.

While, therefore, the sign of circumcision was in every circumcised person, a seal of God's covenant with Abraham and with his seed, it was to all who walked in the faith of Abraham a seal of their personal interest in that same righteousness by which Abraham was justified.

From these general premises the conclusion is direct and irrefragable, that the covenant with Abraham was designed to assure the accomplishment of the second great promise made to him while he was yet in Ur of the Chaldees; and that the effect of it was to bring him and his family, with all who should join them in a kindred profession, *into a church estate,* i. e. was a *covenant ecclesiastical,* by which Jehovah organized the visible church, as one distinct spiritual society; and according to which all his after dealings with her were to be regulated. Hitherto she had been scattered, and existed in detached parts. Now it was the gracious intention of God to reduce her into a compact form that she might be prepared for the good things to come. Since Abraham was designated as the man from whom the MESSIAH was to spring; since he had signally glorified the Lord's veracity, not staggering at his promise through unbelief, he selected this his servant as

the favoured man in whose family he would com-
mence the organization of that church in which
he designed to perpetuate the righteousness of
faith. With this church, as with a *whole*, composed, in the first instance, of Abraham's family,
and to be increased afterwards by the addition of
all such as should own his faith, was the covenant
made. This is that covenant after which we are
inquiring.

II. This covenant has never been annulled.
The proof of the affirmative lies upon the affirm-
er. When? Where? and by whom was the act
for annulling it promulged? The "vanishing
away" of the ceremonial law has nothing to do
with the Abrahamic covenant, but to illustrate,
confirm, and diffuse its blessings. The former
was a temporary constitution superadded for the
purpose of giving effect to some provisions of the
latter, and expired by its own limitation. The
apostle Paul refutes the notion that the introduction of the ceremonial law, could at all prejudice
the pre-existing covenant with Abraham : *Gal.* iii.
15—17. And if not its commencement, why its
termination? And if the abolishing of the ceremonial law does not infer the cessation of the
Abrahamic covenant, there is not a shadow of
either proof or presumption that it has ceased.
If there is, let it be produced. But not to rest
the matter here, we may observe,

1st. That the promise of Abraham's being a father of many nations, who are, therefore, his seed, never was, nor could be fulfilled, before the Christian dispensation. The apostle Paul was certainly of this mind; for he proves the calling of the Gentiles from Abraham's covenant; and if the calling of the Gentiles to be fellow-heirs in the church of God with the literal descendants of the patriarch, was grounded upon his covenant, this, again, shows that they belong to that seed with whom it was made; and, consequently, that it is in full force and virtue at this hour. The apostle presses this point with great ardour; and places it before us in various lights. *If ye be Christ's,* says he, " *then are ye Abraham's seed, and heirs according to the promise.*" What promise? Not simply the promise of eternal life in Christ. There was no *necessity* of their being Abraham's seed to inherit this promise—but manifestly, the promise of Abraham's covenant to which they were entitled in virtue of their being his seed: i. e. the promise, *I will be a God unto thee and to thy seed after thee.* If, then, they who are Christ's are Abraham's seed; and being so are heirs according to the promise; the covenant, containing the promise, is in full virtue, as they belong to the seed with which it was made.

2d. If the Abrahamic covenant is no longer in force, the church of God, as a visible public society, is not, in any sense, connected with him by covenant relation. This may weigh light with those who discard the doctrine of a visible Catholic church; but it draws much deeper than they suspect. The whole administration of the covenant of grace proceeds upon the principle that there *is* such a church. All the ordinances are given to it; all the promises are made to it. To the elect, as such, they are not, cannot be given. The application of them would be impossible without a special revelation : and the whole administration of the covenant of grace, by visible means, would be at an end. Nor is a single instance to be found, excepting in virtue of immediate revelation, in which the Lord ever gave an ordinance or a promise to particular churches. They always receive their privileges in virtue of their being parts of the church universal. Now this church universal, which is the body of Christ, the temple of his Spirit, the depository of his grace, stands in no covenant relation to God, in her public character, if the covenant with Abraham is annulled. For if she does, then another covenant has been made with her. But no such covenant has been made. The new covenant which the Lord promised to make with her at the introduction of the evangelical dispensation, was to supersede, not the Abrahamic, but .the Sinai-covenant. It is so far from setting aside, that it implies, and establishes the former ; for it is promised to her as that church which was organized and perpetuated under Abraham's covenant. If, therefore, that covenant is removed, and no other has replaced it, the church, in her social capacity, is further off from God than she was under the law; and all the mercies to which, in that capacity, she once had a claim, are swept away. But this is impossible. In fact, the scriptures uniformly suppose the existence of such public federal relations: and abound with promises growing out of them. Thus speaks the prophet—" The Redeemer shall come to Zion, and unto them that turn from transgression in Jacob, saith the Lord. As for me, this is my *covenant with them*, saith the Lord : my Spirit that is upon thee, and my words which I have put in thy mouth, shall not depart out of thy mouth, nor out of the mouth of thy seed, nor out of the mouth of thy seed's seed, saith the Lord, from henceforth and for ever."—*Is.* lix. 21, 22.

This is a prediction of New Testament times : so the apostle applies it, *Rom.* xi. 26. And he applies it to the recovery of the Jews, which has not yet happened. The covenant, therefore, is in force, and it operates through the medium of Gentile converts; the Lord's Spirit has long ago departed out of the mouth of the Jews. But the promise was made to the church, in her *covenanted*

character; her members in constant succession
are the " seed" out of whose mouth the divine
Spirit shall not depart; and when the Jews are
restored, they will be brought into this very covenanted church, and be again recognized as a part
of the " seed." But why multiply words ? There
is no explaining the frequent recurrence of the
inspired writers to the covenant of Abraham, nor
any propriety in their reasoning, if it is not of perpetual operation.

3d. In discussing the great question concerning
the rejection of the Jews, the vocation of the
Gentiles, and the future restoration of the former,
the apostle reasons upon principles which are
most false and impertinent, if the Abrahamic covenant has ceased. *Rom.* xi. 17—24.

He tells the Gentiles, that they were " a wild
olive tree;" and that the Jews were the " good
olive tree"—This cannot refer to their natural
state as sinners before God; for in this respect
there was " no difference"—nor to their state as
sinners saved by grace : for from this state there
is no excision; it can refer to nothing but their
visible *church estate;* i. e. to their public relation
to God as a covenanted society. What, then, was
this " good olive tree," from which the Jewish
branches were " broken off;" while the Gentiles
were " graffed in ?" Evidently the visible church
organized under the covenant made with Abra-

ham. There was no other from which the Jews
could be cast off. The ceremonial law was su-
perseded. It was no excision at all to be cut off
from a church which did not exist; nor could
the Gentiles be introduced into it. But what says
the apostle ? That the " olive tree" was cut down
or rooted up ? That it had withered trunk and
branch ? Or was no longer the care of the divine
planter ? Nothing like it ! He asserts the continuance of the olive tree in life and vigour; the excision of some worthless branches; and the insertion
of new ones in their stead. " Thou," says he,
addressing the Gentile, " partakest of the root
and fatness of the olive tree." Translate this into
less figurative language, and what is the import ?
That the church of God, his visible church, taken
into peculiar relations to himself by the Abrahamic covenant, subsists without injury through
the change of dispensation and of members.
Branches indeed may be cut off, but the rooted
trunk stands firm, and other branches occupy the
places of those which are lopped away. The
Jews are cast out of the church, but the church
perished not with them. There was still left the
trunk of the olive tree; there was still fatness in
its roots: it stands in the same fertile soil, the covenant of God: and the admission of the Gentiles
into the room of the excommunicated Jews,
makes them a part of that covenanted church;

as branches graffed into the olive tree and flourish-
ing in its fatness, are identified with the tree. It
is impossible for ideas conceived by the mind of
man, or uttered in his language, to assert more
peremptorily the continuance of the church under
that very covenant which was established with
Abraham and his seed. And this doctrine, understood before the apostleship of Paul, was
maintained by John the Baptist; " *Think not,*"
cried he to the multitudes who crowded around
him, " *think not to say within yourselves, We have
Abraham to our father : for verily I say unto you, that
God is able of these stones to raise up children unto
Abraham.*" The hearers of the Baptist, like many
modern professors of Christianity, supposed that
the duration of the covenant with Abraham, and
of the prerogative of the Jews as God's peculiar
people, were the same. It is a mistake, replies
the second Elijah ; you may all be cast off; you
may all perish ; but the oath to Abraham shall not
be violated. God will be at no loss to provide
" seed" who shall be as much within his covenant
as yourself, even though he should create them
out of the stones of the earth. The threat was
vain: it was empty noise ; it was turning the
thunders of God into a scarecrow for children, if
the covenant with Abraham was not to survive
the law of peculiarity, and be replenished with
other seed than that which sprung from his loins
according to the flesh.

CHURCH OF GOD.

No. III.

On the mode of perpetuating the Visible Church.

IT has been shown, in the preceding number, tnat the covenant with Abraham and his seed, was an *ecclesiastical* covenant; i. e. was made with the *visible church*, and is of equal duration. We proceed to another and very important part of our inquiry. *How were the covenant character and privilege to be transmitted from one age to another, till the consummation of all things ? Or, which is the same, how was a succession of the " seed" to be preserved ?*

This was to be accomplished in two ways.

1st. In all cases of original connexion with the church ; that is, where the individual was without the bond of the covenant, previous to his being of adult age, he was to be admitted on his *personal faith* in that religion which the covenant was instituted to secure, This term of communion with the people of God has never varied. It remains, at the present hour, precisely what it was at the

formation of the Abrahamic covenant. They who
do not enjoy, or have not embraced, the gospel,
are " without." They are " strangers," " foreign-
ers," " aliens," " afar off," and must continue
such till they come to the knowledge of the truth.
No Jewish or Pagan foot must cross the threshold of the church, without " repentance toward
God, and faith toward our Lord Jesus Christ."
About this there is no dispute. About the qualifications requisite in adults for their admission to
the privileges of the church, there is not the same
agreement.

Some think that a general profession of Christianity is all which she may exact; alleging in support of their opinion, the example of the apostles,
who demanded, say they, nothing more than a
confession that *Jesus is the Christ, the Son of God;*
and therefore they conclude that nothing more
ought to be demanded now.

But it is not to be denied that this proposition
contains the substance of all the doctrines and
predictions of the Old Testament, concerning the
Redeemer's person and work. No man could
give it his intelligent assent, without a knowledge
of those doctrines and predictions; nor repose
his hope upon their truth, without that divine faith
which receives the *whole* testimony of God, and
operates, with a purifying influence, upon the
heart and life. The scriptures refer the existence

of such a confession, when not hypocritical, to a much higher cause, and attribute to the confession itself much stronger effects, than are even thought of by those who, at this day, would establish it as the all-comprehending term of Christian fellowship. " I give you to understand," says Paul, 1 Cor. xii. 3. " that no man can say that Jesus is the Lord, but *by the Holy Ghost.*"—And John 1, Ep. v. 1. 5. " Whosoever believeth that Jesus is the Christ, is *born of God.*"—" Who is he that *overcometh the world,* but he that believeth that Jesus is the Son of God." It is evident, upon the very face of these passages, that nothing was further from the mind and the practice of the Apostles, than the recognizing as Christians and the admitting into Christian fellowship, all or any who barely assented to the general proposition, that " Jesus is the Christ." Much less can such an admission be justifiable now, when millions learn, from mere habit, to repeat that proposition without weighing its sense, or even comprehending its terms. Christianity is not a thing of *rote.* And there can be no doubt, that multitudes would flock to the church, reiterating as often as you would wish, their belief that " Jesus is the Christ ;" who should, nevertheless, be found, upon a strict examination, to be either ignorant, or enemies, of every truth comprehended in their own creed. This cannot be. Christianity is not chargeable

with the madness of cherishing in her own bosom,
and that designedly, the seeds of her own
destruction.

Some think that soundness in the doctrines of
revelation, without scrutiny into practical character, or, at least, without solicitude on that point,
is sufficient to justify admission into the church,
and to the enjoyment of her privileges.

This opinion is not more correct than the former. It strips the church of her responsibility on
the score of moral purity; annihilates her duties
with regard to the chief end of her creation; viz.
that she might be the mother of a holy seed, of a
" peculiar people, zealous of good works ;" dis-
severs the connexion between faith in Christ ·and
conformity to his image; and acts, not indeed
upon the notion that provided a man's life be good,
his faith is a matter of indifference; but upon its
converse, equally absurd and abominable, that a
right belief may dispense with the obligations of
holiness.

Some think, that doctrinal soundness combined
with fair morals, fixes the limit of our inquiries.
This opinion, though far preferable to the others,
labours, notwithstanding, under a material defect.
It shuts out investigation of the history of a man's
heart and conscience; in other words, of his religious experience. This must certainly form a
part of his profession which is to be tried by the

rules of the written word. The gospel, if received in truth, has revolutionized his soul. It has taught him to hate sin, his own sin, and to abhor himself for it before God—It has taught him to renounce dependence upon his own righteousness; abjuring it, in every form and degree, as the ground of his acceptance with his judge; to rest, with absolute and exclusive reliance, upon the righteousness of our Lord Jesus Christ; and to live by faith upon him as the Lord his strength. They who have but slightly attended to facts, need not be told that it is very possible, and very common, to have a speculative orthodoxy and an unstained reputation, with as complete an absence of the whole of this spiritual efficacy of the gospel upon the heart, as if no such thing were either mentioned in the bible or existed in our world. And it would be strange indeed, if the church of God, in admitting men to her distinguished privileges, should never ask a question concerning the most glorious and only saving effect of that very gospel which her members are supposed to believe.

Some, in fine, think that religious experience is the sole test of admission into the church. Provided a man can satisfy them of his conversion, and they are not always hard to be satisfied; if he can relate a plausible story of his feelings; can talk of his distress, and of his comfort; and has learnt to deal in joys and ecstacies, it is enough.

How he came by his experience, he probably cannot tell, and his spiritual guides often omit to ask. And yet this is a point upon which often turns the discrimination between true and false in religion; between rational experience and fanaticism; between the good influences of the Spirit of God, and their counterfeits. It is lamentable that so large a proportion of conversions, which are the fruit of tumultuous meetings, and the theme of newspaper praise, prove to be of this class. Dark views, gross ignorance, and even flat contradictions in the simplest truths of Christianity, are no obstacle. Thousands go from sin to God; from nature to grace; from condemnation to pardon; from despondency to rapture; and when interrogated about the *process* by which this marvellous transition was accomplished, have little or nothing to say, but that *they have felt so !* And, what is still more astonishing, they have been "translated from darkness to light," without being illuminated! For the uttering of incoherent exclamations, and the chattering over a set of phrases, though accompanied with vehement passion, with shrieks and fallings, and faintings, and fits, and trances, must not pass for divine illumination, nor divine influence of any sort. When we consider the mechanism of the human affections, and how rapidly emotion is propagated, by sympathy, through promiscuous crowds, we can explain all the phe nomena which, in this matter, have lately attracted the public wonder, without recourse to supernatural agency; and must be convinced that nothing can be more precarious than the tenure by which these sudden converts hold their profession. And although many, to whom, therefore, these remarks will not apply, disclaim that wild frenzy which others have rashly mistaken for an effusion of the divine Spirit, yet it is not easy to make *mere* experience the rule of estimating Christian character, and of admitting to Christian privilege; and at the same time keep clear of extravagances. For let the imagination, freed from the restraint of purified reason, be once excited; let it be impelled by a fervid but blind devotion, and it will rush, with resistless impetuosity, into excesses fit only to dishonour the Christian name, and to desolate the Christian church.—Wherever the understanding is dismissed from religion, nothing but mischief can ensue; and this is always done, in a greater or less degree, where the exercises of the heart are assumed as the basis of our judgment without ascertaining their dependence upon knowledge.

Upon the whole we may conclude, that an adult, in order to his right reception into the Christian church,

Must be acquainted with, at least, the leading doctrines of revelation:

Must be able to " give a reason of the hope that is in him," by showing that these doctrines have operated upon his experience:

Must make an open, unequivocal avowal of the Redeemer's name: and,

Must be vigilant in the habitual discharge of his religious and moral duty.

He, in whom these things meet, is a Christian, and to be recognized as such by the Christian church.

But now arises another question. Does the church, in bringing an adult to the test of the foregoing requisites, and pronouncing him worthy of her communion, act upon the principle of her *discovering* that he is a regenerated person; and that he *really is*, in the sight of God, what he *appears to be* in the sight of men ?

By no means. The church, as conducted by a system of instituted ordinances, which men administer, is altogether *visible ;* and it would be absurd to make an invisible quality the criterion of visible communion.

Our Lord Jesus Christ, who fell into no mistakes, actually did admit an unconverted man, a hypocrite, a traitor, a devil, into the number not only of his disciples, but even of his apostles : thereby instructing his church that the secret state of the soul before God is not to be her rule of judgment. He knew, from the beginning, who should betray him; and yet permitted the infidel to mingle in his train; to continue in his service, to share the honours of his sincere followers; and never cast him off till he had proved his rottenness by an overt act of treachery. All which would have been impossible, had the reality of a gracious condition been the ground of church connexion. And it betrays something very different from modesty to set up a term of religious fellowship which would convict the master himself of corrupting his own church.

God has reserved to himself the prerogative of exploring secret motives. " I, Jehovah, search the heart. I try the reins." And it is a source of ineffable consolation that none but himself *can* try them. The obtrusion of the creature is completely barred out by his own unchangeable constitution. I bless him for it. I had rather perish than have my heart searched by men or angels; and I put them all at defiance to declare what passes in my breast any further than I myself inform them by my own act. Whoever, therefore, maintains that the *reality* of conversion is the reason of admission to Christian privilege, lays down a rule which never can be applied. There are none who furnish more conclusive evidence of its nullity, than those who most warmly contend for it. A single observation will put this in a strong light. They who, without the aid of a revelation either

from myself or my creator, can read my hidden
thoughts on one occasion, can read them on every
other. Therefore, if they can ascertain sincerity
in religion they can equally ascertain it in their
civil transactions; and consequently would never
be imposed upon. But to such lengths they do
not pretend to go; that is, they proclaim the
falsity of their own doctrine, and the futility of
their own rule. How dare they who cannot detect a perjury in the custom-house, or a lie in the
shop, represent themselves as able to detect hypocrisy in religious profession? It is foolish conceit; it is contemptible quackery. Take notice
how they use their own rule. They get a man to
recount his experience. If satisfied with that,
they set him down as converted. You see, that
for the facts on which they build their judgment,
they have only his own word; and yet they talk
of ascertaining his state! Two plain questions on
this head, and we shall leave them :

If their man should say nothing at all, how
would they find out his state?

If he should happen to amuse them with a tale
of experience such as they approve, and he never
felt, where is their *knowledge* of his state?

As for those who undertake to *discern spirits*,
without producing their authority from the father
of spirits, under his broad seal of miracles, nothing is so amazing about them as their effrontery.

All sober men should eschew them as jugglers and impostors. An astrologer who cast nativities from the aspect of the planets; or a strolling gipsey who predicts the history of life from the palm of a child's hand, is as worthy of credence as they.

The result is, that when, according to our best judgment, we perceive those things which are the known and regular effects of Christian principle, we are to account their possessor a brother, and to embrace him accordingly. In other words, *a credible profession of Christianity*, is all that the church may require in order to communion. She may be deceived; her utmost caution may be, and often has been, ineffectual to keep bad men from her sanctuary. And this, too, without her fault, as she is not omniscient. But she has no right to suspect sincerity, to refuse privilege, or to inflict censure, where she can put her finger upon nothing repugnant to the love or the laws of God.

It must of necessity be so. For the principle now laid down is inseparable from human nature, and pervades every form of human society. Examine them all, from the great commonwealth of the nation down to the petty club, and you will meet with no exception. When an alien becomes a citizen, he takes an oath of allegiance to the government. When one becomes a member of a

literary, a mechanical, a benevolent, or any other
association, he accedes to its constitution and
rules.   These are their *professions* respectively.
They may profess falsely: But that is nothing to
the society, so long as the falsehood is locked up
within their own breasts: They are accounted,
and rightly accounted, " good men and true," till
they forfeit their reputation and their immunities
by some criminal deed.   Who doubts that individuals unfaithful in heart to their engagements,
are scattered through all these combinations?
Yet who would deem it better than madness to
decide on their external relations without a warrant from external acts ? What horrible confusion
would follow a departure from this maxim? Nothing can be true which contradicts any of the
great analogies of God's works; nor can his
church be established by the operation of a principle which, in every other case, would destroy all
confidence and intercourse among men.

A profession, then, of faith in Christ, and of
obedience to him, not discredited by other traits
of character, entitles an adult to the privileges of
his church.   And this is the first way of securing
a succession of the covenanted seed, and of hand-
ing down their blessings to the end of time.

But the *second* and principal channel of convey-
ance is *hereditary descent*. The relations and benefits of the covenant are the *birthright* of every

child born of parents who are themselves of " the seed." " I will establish," says God, " my covenant between me and thee, and *thy seed after thee, in their generations,* for an everlasting covenant." The substance of which, to repeat a preceding proposition, manifestly is, that as soon as a new individual is generated from this seed, he is within the covenant, and, according to its tenour, God is his God. This is a characteristic of every public covenant which God has made with man. Take, for example, the covenants with Adam and with Noah. Every human creature comes into being under the full operation of both these covenants. In virtue of the one, he is an " heir of wrath ;" and in virtue of the other, an heir of promise to the whole extent of the covenant-mercy. He has the faithfulness of God pledged to him, as one of Noah's covenanted seed, that the world shall not be drowned by a second deluge ; nor visited by another calamity to exterminate his race

Now, what imaginable reason can be assigned, why, in the covenant with his visible church, the uniform and consistent God should depart from his known rule of dispensation, and violate all the natural and moral analogies of his works and his government? It cannot be. There is no such violation; there is no such departure. Nor is it so much as pretended to have happened from Abraham till John the Baptist, or perhaps the day

of Pentecost. But what was in the ministry of
the Baptist? What in the ministry of Jesus
Christ? What in the effusion of the Holy Spirit
at Pentecost, to destroy a radical principle of that
very church which John, and Jesus, and the Spirit
of Jesus, were sent to bless and perfect? The
notion is wild. And if, as has been already demonstrated, the covenant with Abraham and his
seed was a covenant with the visible church—if
this covenant has never been abrogated—if its relations and privileges, with an exception in favour
of adults who desired to come in on the profession
of their faith, were to be propagated in the line of
natural generation, THEN, it follows, that the infant
seed of persons who are under this covenant, are
themselves parties to it; are themselves members
of the church; and whatever privileges that infant
seed had, at any given period in the history of the
church, it *must retain* so long as the covenant is in
force. But the covenant is in force at this moment;
therefore, at this moment, the covenant privileges
of the infant seed are in force. Visible membership is one of those privileges; therefore the infant seed of church members are also members
of the church.

However men may corrupt and have corrupted
the ordinance of God, so as to reject the visible
means which he has appointed for perpetuating
his church, yet as they cannot overset his govern-

ment, they are compelled to see the principle here contended for, operating, with irresistible force, every hour before their eyes. For whether they will, or whether they will not, the fact is, that the church of God, with an exception before mentioned, ever has been, and is now, propagated by hereditary descent. There is not, perhaps, in any nation under heaven that has been once christianized, and has not sinned away the gospel, a single Christian who has not received his privileges as an inheritance from his fathers. Let us then beware how, in opposing infant church membership, we fight against a principle which is wrought into the essence of all God's constitutions respecting

CHURCH OF GOD.

No. IV.

Initiating Seal.

ON the " sign of circumcision" which God an-
nexed to his covenant with Abraham, as " a seal
of the righteousness of faith," some remarks have
already been made. In its immediate reference
to the Patriarch's seed, it certified that they belonged to the church of God, and were entitled
to all the privileges which she derived immediately from the covenant with their great progenitor.
A right to this seal, was the *birthright* of every
Hebrew; and it was accordingly applied to him
when he was eight days old. That this right was
not peculiar to the literal, but was common to
the covenanted, seed, is clear from the case of
proselytes, who having cleaved to the God of
Abraham, were themselves circumcised, and imparted to their children all the prerogatives of a
native Hebrew.

On the supposition, then, that circumcision had

not been laid aside, as the covenant, of which it
was the seal, has not, it would be at this hour
the duty of professing parents to circumcise their
infant sons; that is, to have an interest in God's
covenant certified to their seed, by applying the
seal of it to their male infants. Circumcision,
however, having been discontinued, the question
is, whether the seal which it conveyed has been
discontinued with it ? If so, then these two consequences follow.

First, That there is no longer any initiatory
seal for adults, any more than for infants; because
an *abolished* seal can no more be applied to a
man than to a babe; and thence,

Secondly, That the church of God is under the
operation of an *unsealed covenant*; that is, that
God has withdrawn the sensible pledge of his covenant relation to her. If it be said that Baptism
is appointed to be the initiatory seal under the
New Testament dispensation, and is directed to
be applied to believing adults, the plea is true;
but it concedes much more than suits the purpose
of many who urge it.

(1.) As a seal must certify something; as no
seal was ever ordained by God but as the seal of
his covenant; and as no wise man will pretend
that every lawfully baptized adult, is undoubtedly
within the covenant of grace, it concedes that God
has a visible church in sealed covenant with himself,

distinct from that church which is composed of the elect only.

(2.) As he has never made a *new visible church ;* nor drawn back from his old engagements, this plea concedes, that the church now in existence is the very church organized by the Abrahamic covenant ; and that covenant the very one which is sealed to her by baptism.   Then,

(3.) That baptism has come in the place of circumcision ; and as adults are ordered to be baptized, without a syllable of the exclusion of infants, the application of circumcision must furnish the rule for that of baptism.   And consequently, this same plea which is designed to preclude infant baptism, turns out to be a demonstration of its divine right.   Thus the point before us would be completely settled.   But to wave this advantage, and to put the subject in another light, let us distinguish, in this matter of circumcision, between the substance and form.   The substance of the ordinance, that which properly constituted the *seal*, was the certification to the person sealed, of his interest in God's covenant.   The rite of circumcision was no more than the *form* in which the seal was applied.   These two things must not be confounded.   For, on the one hand, the *rite* may be, and was, and is yet, performed without any sealing whatever.   The sons of Ishmael were circumcised, but they belonged not to

the covenanted seed, and therefore circumcision
sealed nothing to them.   The Jews are circumcised still, but being cut off from the olive-tree, being cast out of the church of God, and suspended
from the privileges of the covenanted seed, their
circumcision is nothing.   On the other hand, the
seal had been the same, although administered by
a different rite. The amputation of a toe, the per-
foration of an ear, the sprinkling of blood, or the
anointing with oil, would have answered the purpose as well as circumcision.   The essence of the
seal lying not in the *rite*, but in the divine sanction
which is given by that rite to claims on God's covenant.   Now as it is self-evident, that this sanction may be conveyed under any form which he
shall please to prescribe, it is a gross errour in
reasoning to conclude, that because the ancient
form is laid aside, therefore the seal and all things
certified by it are laid aside too.   It would be
quite as accurate to infer, that because the form
of church polity is altered, therefore the church
no longer exists.   If it be objected, that " however distinguishable the seal and the sealing rite
be from each other in theory, they are inseparable in fact; as the former cannot be applied to us
but through the medium of the latter; and therefore if this be abolished, the other is to us as if it
did not exist;" I reply, that the objection con-
cludes equally against the existence of a church

upon earth; for it must appear in some visible form, or else, *to us*, it is no church : and the argument is still good, that if the abolition of a particular form of sealing God's covenant, involves the abolition of the seal itself, then the abolition of a particular form of his church, involves the abolition of the church itself. The objection assumes the very point in debate, viz. that the seal of the covenant and a particular form of the sealing rite are co-existent, and perish together. Whereas it is contended, that the cessation of the latter does by no means imply the cessation of the former; but that the seal may remain the same, although the rite be changed; and may pass, in its full virtue and efficacy, through successive forms of application. In truth, it is a fundamental principle, that *forms of dispensation do not affect the substance of the things dispensed.* Otherwise, the covenant of grace has been changed often. But if *five* forms of dispensation have not touched the substance of the covenant of grace; nor *three* forms of dispensation, the substance of the covenant with Abraham; why should the disuse of a particular mode of sealing this latter, draw after it the destruction of the seal itself? and of all the relations and benefits sealed ? The issue is, that circumcision may be laid aside without infringing upon the covenant to which it was appended. It has been laid aside, and the question is, What has been

substituted in its place?   As none of the parties
to this controversy pretend that it has been succeeded by any other ordinance than baptism, the
only alternative is, either that nothing at all has
been substituted for it, or else that the substitute
is baptism.

If nothing—then while the covenant is in force,
and a covenant which must be sealed too, there
is no method of applying the seal.

If nothing—then a privilege has been taken
away from the church, and she has received no
compensation; contrary to the whole tenour of
God's dealing with her, and to the positive declarations of his word.

If nothing—then the apostle Peter led his hearers astray, in assuring them that the " promise
was to them and their children," which, as Jews,
they could not understand of any other promise
than that made to Abraham ; nor in any other
sense, than as asserting the joint interest of their
infants, with themselves, in the covenant of God,
and, consequently, their right to the seal of that
interest.   One of the most stubborn and rational
prejudices of the Jews against the Christian dispensation, was the fear of losing the privileges to
which, as Abraham's seed, they had a covenant
claim; and which they, with better excuse than
Christians *now*, supposed to be inseparable from
the law of Moses. " You mistake the matter,"

cries Peter, full of the Holy Ghost, " there is nothing in the gospel of Jesus Christ, nor the new
economy which he has introduced, to destroy or
abridge the mercies held out and secured by the
covenant with Abraham. The Saviour is, himself, the chief blessing of that covenant. The
evangelical dispensation displays its provisions
in clearer light, and greater extent. The promise subsists in unabated virtue, and with increased glory ; it is, at this moment, as much
as at any moment past, *to you and to your children ;*
but it is also to *all them that are afar off, even as
many as the Lord your God shall call.*" How could
the words of Peter be interpreted by a Jew ? In
no other way than this, that neither the covenant
of Abraham, nor the seal of that covenant, nor
the interest of his infant seed in it was abrogated,
or to be abrogated, by the Christian dispensation.
How could they be interpreted by a Gentile ? In
no other way than this, that persons who " were
afar off," (the very phrase by which Paul describes
the Gentiles,) being called by the gospel, should
come into the full possession of all the benefits
which are contained in the covenant with Abraham;
that is, should enjoy, equally with the Jew, whatever, according to the nature of that covenant, is
comprehended in the declaration, *I will be thy God,
and the God of thy seed ;* and equally with the Jew,
the pledge and seal of this his privilege. The

Apostle speaks of a promise well-known and high-
ly prized. " *The* promise," without any explanation. " What promise ?" inquires the Gentile.
Ask your brother, the Jew, rejoins the Apostle;
he understands me thoroughly. It is the promise
made to his father, Abraham; that in *his seed all
the nations of the earth shall be blessed.* " True,"
you will interrupt, " this is the Apostle's meaning, and it says not a syllable of circumcision, nor
of its relation to baptism ; nor of infant church
membership." Yes, but is a promise in Abraham's covenant : it depends upon the immuta-
bility of that covenant. For no engagement
whatever, can survive the covenant which gives it
birth and validity. And this very promise, the
Holy Ghost being judge, was to be so fulfilled,
that the blessing of Abraham might come upon
the Gentiles; which must mean that they and
their seed should be admitted to the privileges
granted to Abraham and his seed: so that the
children of professing Christians, not less than
themselves, should be within the covenant, and
entitled to its seal. Thus the Jews evidently understood the Apostle; for among all their objections to the Christian system, they never objected
the *exclusion of their infant seed from the church of
God.* If, therefore, nothing has come in the place
of circumcision, the Apostle acted disingenuously
with his Jewish hearers ; and quieted their appre-

hension by a fraud upon their consciences. The fraud extended to the Gentile converts; for it referred them to the Jewish standard of interpretation; and every one of the inspired penmen of the New Testament is accessary to its influence, as there is not a sentence in all their writings to correct the errour; and the deception will not end even with *them*—*******!

But if these things cannot be maintained—If there is no such mockery as a seal without a mode of sealing, and the primitive form of circumcision is abolished—If God has not stripped his church of a privilege, without giving her an equivalent—If the holy Apostle did not abuse the understanding of his hearers, nor sport with their faith in his veracity—then is baptism the substitute for circumcision.

But as this conclusion may be thought too strong for the general argument preceding it, let us submit it to a more direct proof, by inquiring into the scriptural account of both circumcision and baptism. And, *First*, let us see how this account stands with regard to them *separately*. It will be seen in the following contrast.

CIRCUMCISION,	BAPTISM,
1. Was an initiatory rite, by which the circumcised were owned as of the covenanted seed, and of the people of God.	1. Is an initiatory rite, by which the baptized are numbered among the disciples of Christ, and the members of the church of God.

2. Was a seal of the righteousness of faith. Rom. iv. 11. i. e. of the Justification of a sinner through the righteousness of the surety embraced by faith.

2. The person is baptized in the name of Jesus Christ for the remission of sins, (Act. ii. 38.) which is through faith in his blood; so that God is just and the justifier of him that believeth in Jesus.

3. Was an emblem and a means of internal sanctity. *The Lord thy God will circumcise thine heart, and the heart of thy seed, to love the Lord thy God with all thine heart, and with all thy soul, that thou mayest live.* Deut. xxx. 6. See also ch. x. 16.

3. Is a sign and means of our sanctification in virtue of our communion with Christ.—*Buried with him by baptism into death; that like as Christ was raised up from the dead by the glory of the Father, even so we also should walk in newness of life.* Rom. vi. 4. See also 1 Pet. iii. 21.

The parallel is certainly striking : Circumcision and baptism do both put a mark upon their subjects, as belonging to that society which God hath set apart for himself. They both signify and seal that wondrous change in the state of a sinner, whereby, being justified by faith, he passes from condemnation into acceptance with God; which doctrines of pardon and acceptance are exhibited in that society alone, which, under the name of his church, God hath consecrated to himself, and of which he hath appointed the circumcised and baptized to be esteemed members. Both represent, and are means of obtaining, that real purity which is effected by the spirit of Christ; and is the characteristic of all those members of his church who are justified by faith in his blood. Such a coincidence cannot be casual. It bespeaks design. And seeing that circumcision and baptism do thus substantially answer the same ends, and that the former has ceased, the only sound conclusion is, that it has been succeeded by the latter. Change of dispensation was a sufficient reason why the form of sealing the covenant dispensed should also be changed; and the points of difference between baptism and circumcision, as covenant seals, are only such as were demanded by the nature of the change: the former being much better adapted to a more extensive and spiritual dispensation than the latter. And this is an additional consideration to show that the one has been substituted in the room of the other.

Let us proceed in our inquiry by examining, *Secondly*, into the scriptural manner of representing circumcision and baptism when they are spoken of *together ;* or when baptism is mentioned in connexion with the covenant of which circumcision was the seal.—Take two examples.

1. The Apostle Peter, in his famous address to which there has already been frequent reference, assigns the perpetuity of Abraham's covenant, and the validity of its promise, as a reason why his Jewish hearers should be *baptized*. *Repent*, says he, *and be baptized every one of you, in the name of*

Jesus Christ, for the remission of sins, and ye shall receive the gift of the Holy Ghost; for the promise is unto you and to your children. But how could this promise, being still assured to them and to their children, be a reason for their baptism in the name of Jesus Christ, unless baptism were a seal of that same promise as exhibited in the new economy ? " Your circumcision sealed to you," says the Apostle, " your interest in the covenant with Abraham, as it was exhibited under the law : baptism seals your interest in that covenant, as it is exhibited in perfection under the Gospel. If you refuse the Lord Jesus, and the initiating ordinance of his dispensation, you refuse the better things which God has provided for you. If you yield yourselves up to the Lord Jesus Christ, you will have all that the promise contains in its application to this better state of things, sealed unto you ; *therefore*, repent and be baptized." In this view, the argument is conclusive. In any other, it is of no force at all. What persuasion to baptism could there be in the consideration that the promise was to them and their children, if baptism had no relation to the promise? and what relation could it have unless as a seal, occupying the same place with regard to the promise under the new dispensation, which was occupied by circumcision under the old ? Admitting this, every thing is clear. Two initiatory rites of the same general import, cannot exist together. The dispensation by Christ Jesus takes place of the dispensation by Abraham, with all the additions by Moses; the form of sealing the covenant under this, takes place of the form of sealing it under those. The greater contains all that was contained in the less, and supersedes it. Baptism supplants circumcision.

2. In the epistle of Paul to the Colossians, is the following passage. "*In whom,*" viz. Christ, "*also ye are* CIRCUMCISED *with the* CIRCUMCISION *made without hands, in putting off the* BODY OF THE SINS OF THE FLESH, *by the* CIRCUMCISION OF CHRIST; *buried with him in* BAPTISM, *wherein also ye are* RISEN *with him, through the faith of the operation of God, who hath raised him from the dead.*" Chap. ii. **11, 12.**

This is a very extensive proposition, made up of a number of subordinate ones which it is necessary distinctly to weigh.

1st. Both circumcision and baptism are to be viewed as signs of *spiritual mercies.* It is for this reason alone, that they are or can be employed as *terms* to convey the idea of such mercies.

2d. Circumcision was a sign of regeneration, and of communion with Christ, as the fountain of spiritual life. The apostle is treating of a believer's *completeness in Christ*—of *circumcision in Christ.* That his meaning might not be mistaken, he explains himself of the *inward grace,* calling it,

" the *circumcision made without hands,*" and to cut off all misconception, he explains his explanation, declaring this " circumcision without hands," to be, *the putting off the body of the sins of the flesh, by the circumcision of Christ.*

3d. Baptism, too, is a sign of regeneration, and of communion with Christ, as the fountain of spiritual life.

In baptism, saith Paul, ye are "buried *with Christ,*" " ye are risen *with him,*" through a divine faith, " the faith of the operation of God."—Whereas ye were " dead in sins, and the *uncircumcision of your flesh,*" (uncircumcision put for the state of irregeneracy,) God hath *quickened you together with Christ.*

Collect now the result. A believer's sanctification, in virtue of union with Christ, Paul declares to be represented by both circumcision and baptism; for he expresses his doctrine by these terms indifferently; and annexes to them both, the same spiritual signification. He has, therefore, *identified* the two ordinances : and thus, by demonstrating that they have one and the same use and meaning, he has exhibited to our view the very same seal of God's covenant, under the forms of circumcision and baptism respectively. But as the same thing cannot subsist in different forms at the same time : and as the first form, viz. circumcision, is laid aside; it follows, that the seal of God's covenant is perpetuated under the second form, viz. baptism; and that it signifies and seals in a manner suited to the evangelical dispensation, whatever was previously signified and sealed by the rite of circumcision.

If we again inspect the Apostle's proposition, we shall find, that he directs us to this conclusion, as well by the structure of his phraseology, as by the force of his argument. For, on the one hand, by the indiscriminate use of the terms circumcision and baptism, he appears to assume, as an indisputable fact, the substitution of the latter in place of the former; nor is it easy to conceive why he should discourse in this allusive manner, if the exchange were not perfectly understood among Christians: and, on the other hand, his language is so framed, as to assert that exchange. "Circumcised—in putting off the body of the sins of the flesh, by the *circumcision of Christ;* buried with him in *baptism.*" What can the apostle intend, by the "*circumcision* of Christ?" Doubtless, not the literal rite, for this would destroy at once the whole of his reasoning on the article of sanctification, in the same way as it is destroyed by those who interpret the phrase, "buried with him in baptism," of submersion of the body in the act of baptising. The apostle cannot so trifle. By the "circumcision of Christ," he means that righteousness of faith, that mortification of sin, that quickening influence, which flow from Christ, and were signified by circumcision. But that same righteousness of faith, and mortification of sin, and quickening influence, are also signified by baptism. But circumcision and baptism are external signs, which the apostle recognizes by specifying the things signified. In his transition from the one to the other, that is, from circumcision to baptism, as signifying, in their respective places, the very same blessings, he points to the transition which the church of God has made in fact, from the use of the former to the use of the latter. " With regard to the things signified," saith he, " there is no difference. The circumcision of Christ, and burial with him in baptism, are expressions of similar import; both declaring a believer's communion with him in his covenant mercies. With regard to the outward sign, fellowship with Christ in his death and resurrection, is represented in baptism, as putting off the body of " the sins of the flesh," was formerly represented in circumcision." If this be just, the inference is plain. Baptism is the *Christian* circumcision; the sign of baptism is the *Christian* form of sealing God's covenant, and, as such, has taken place of circumcision.

In confirmation of what is here advanced, let us look, for a moment, at the Apostle's account of Abraham's circumcision; Rom. iv. 11, &c. *He*

*received the sign of circumcision, a seal of the right-
eousness of the faith which he had, yet being uncircumcised; that he might be the father of all them
that believe, though they be not circumcised; that
righteousness might be imputed unto them also. And
the father of circumcision to them who are not of the
circumcision only, but who also walk in the steps of
that faith of our father Abraham, which he had, being
yet uncircumcised.*

Two great prerogatives are here ascribed to
Abraham:

1. That he should transmit, in the line of the
covenanted seed, the righteousness of faith to all
generations and nations, so as to be, in a sense
which belonged, and could belong, to no other
man, the *Father of all them that believe.*

2. That with the righteousness of faith, he
should transmit the seal of God's covenant, by the
intervention of which it was to be perpetuated in
the world, and actually imputed to all believers.
For he was not only the father of all them that
believe, but " the father of *circumcision*" to them.

This cannot mean the things *signified* by circumcision; for the apostle includes them in the
first prerogative: and such an interpretation would
convert into mere tautology, two propositions
which are strongly distinguished from each other
in the text. Circumcision, says the apostle, was
a seal of the righteousness of the faith which Abra

ham had before he was circumcised: and he is
the father of this circumcision to all them who
walk in the steps of his faith; that is, he transmits
the sign and seal along with the thing signified;
conveying the evidence of God's covenant, as far
and as wide as he conveys the blessing ministered
by it, so that in whatever sense he is the father
of them that believe, in the same sense is he the
father to them of the seal of that righteousness
which they embrace by faith: and further, the
benefits conferred through the medium of Abraham's covenant, are asserted to be contemporary
with the seal; both descending together from
him to the last of the covenanted seed. The
Apostle himself applies the principle, in the most
positive terms, to the old and the new dispensation.

To the old dispensation—" The father of circumcision to them who are not of the circumcision
only," evidently those who, being his descendants,
or incorporated with them, were literally circumcised. They inherited the seal from their father
Abraham. This is not questioned. But the
Apostle extends the principle.

To the new dispensation—The " father of circumcision to them also who walk in the steps of
his faith." In what sense is Abraham the " father
of circumcision," as the Apostle maintains, to
them who never were literally circumcised, and

whom he expressly distinguishes from the circumcision? Manifestly in this sense, that they, being accounted of Abraham's seed, by their admission into the church of God, receive along with it, by inheritance from the patriarch, the seal of that covenant in which they are become interested. But circumcision is abolished long ago: yet Abraham is the father of circumcision to them at this hour. There is no avoiding a direct contradiction, but upon the principle, that though the outward rite of circumcision be discontinued, yet the substance of the ordinance, the seal of the covenant abides; is applied under another form, and is as really inherited by the people of God from their father Abraham in that form, as it was inherited by them of old in the form of circumcision. But now, if this seal does not subsist in the ordinance of baptism, it has no existence at all; and there is no possible sense in which Abraham is *to us* the father of circumcision. Therefore, baptism has succeeded to circumcision.

This reasoning draws after it, infallibly, the church membership of infants, and their right to baptism. For as there is no distinction between the mode in which Abraham has handed down the sealed privileges of God's covenant to those who were, and those who were not, of the circumcision; and as they were made over to the former, and their infant seed, they must also be made

over to the latter and their infant seed.   It is no
objection to the foregoing argument, that baptism
is administered to *female* infants, whereas only
males were circumcised : because the *extension* of
a privilege can never be pleaded as a proof of its
abrogation ; and the New Testament itself has positively annulled, in spiritual things, all pre-eminence and inferiority arising from condition or
sex.

The only difficulty of any importance, under
which the doctrine of these pages can labour, is
the application of the seal of the righteousness of
faith to multitudes who never had and never will
have that righteousness ;   consequently, that the
seal of God's covenant, who is the God of truth,
is, by his own appointment, very often affixed to
a lie.

The difficulty is precisely the same in reference to circumcision as to baptism.   The former was undoubtedly " a seal of the righteousness of faith;" and as undoubtedly was often
applied to multitudes who never had that righteousness.   Did the God of truth, therefore, *certify a lie ?* Methinks so blasphemous a deduction, which is equally valid against his *acknowledged* institution of infant circumcision, as against
his *disputed* institution of infant baptism, should
make sober men, who cannot escape from it,
suspect. the soundness of their views.   It is, more-

over, the same difficulty which occurs in the cele-
bration of the Lord's supper, and in the baptism
of adults; unless we can be assured that *all* the
recipients are *true converts.* But, indeed, the difficulty itself is created by erroneous notions of the
nature of God's church; by confounding visible
members with his elect—and his covenant to the
church, with his covenant of grace in Christ Jesus.
A proper application of this distinction will remove it, and *demonstrate that the seal of God's covenant, does, in every instance, certify absolute truth,
whether it be applied to a believer, or to an unbeliever ;
to the elect, or to the reprobate.*

CHURCH OF GOD.

No. V.

Infant members.

In our preceding numbers, we have given a
general view of the Church of God, as one great
visible society which he has taken into peculiar
relations to himself. We traced its origin, as an
organized whole, up to the Abrahamic covenant, of
which we explained the nature, and proved the
perpetuity. We also investigated the uses of its
initiating rite, viz. circumcision; which, we assigned reasons to show, has been exchanged, under the evangelical dispensation, for the ordinance
of baptism : and we touched, in general terms,
upon the conclusion which our premises justify,
respecting the ecclesiastical condition and privileges of infants born of believing parents. Having avowed our pursuasion, that they are, in virtue of their birth, members of the church of God,
and entitled, during their infancy, to baptism in
his name, we shall, in this number, state our con-

clusion more fully, and shall strengthen it with some auxiliary considerations.

The reader, on looking back to No. III. of this series, will find the following paragraph.

" If, as has been already demonstrated, the covenant with Abraham and his seed was a covenant with the visible church—if this covenant has never been abrogated—if its relations and privileges, with an exception in favour of adults who desired to come in on the profession of their faith, were to be propagated in the line of natural generation, THEN, it follows, that the infant seed of persons who are under this covenant, are themselves parties to it ; are themselves members of the church ; and whatever privileges that infant seed had at any given period in the history of the church, it *must retain* so long as the covenant is in force.   But the covenant is in force at this moment ; therefore, at this moment, the covenant privileges of the infant seed are in force.   Visible membership is one of those privileges ; therefore the infant seed of church members are also members of the church."

This, then, is the ground on which we take our stand in pleading the cause of the children whom God has given us.   We account them members of his church, not, because *tradition* has called them so ; not because the *practice* of the church has treated them as such ; but because he constituted them such by his own commandment and covenant which he has never revoked until this day.

To insist, therefore, that we shall produce, from the New Testament, a precept directly instituting the church membership of infants, is to make a demand with which we are under no obligation to comply. Such a precept was not necessary. The relation we are inquiring into had been instituted long before ; it had subsisted without one moment's interruption for more than nineteen centuries. During this great lapse of ages it had enlisted on its side, in addition to its divine original, the most irrefragable prejudices of antiquity, the most confirmed national habit, and the fastidious jealousy of prerogative. In this state of its prevalence was the evangelical dispensation announced. If the same relation of infants to the church was to continue under the New Testament form, nothing is more easy than to assign the reason why it was not instituted anew. The principle was undisputed ; it was acted upon as a principle which the change of dispensation did not touch ; and consequently, a new institution was superfluous. The silence of the New Testament on this head, is altogether in favour of those who maintain that the union of parents with the church of God, includes their children also. But on the supposition that this principle was to

operate no longer ; that the common interest of
children with their parents in God's covenant was
to cease ; the silence of the New Testament is
one of the most inexplicable things which ever
tortured the ingenuity of man. If there is any
point of external privilege which ought to have
been settled with the most definite precision, one
would imagine that this is the point. But we are
taught to believe, that a constitution which is en-
grafted upon a principle that penetrates the essence of human society ; which coincides with
the genius of every other divine constitution respecting man ; which is incorporated with his
animal, his intellectual, and his moral character ;
which is interwoven with every ligament and fibre
of his heart, shall be torn away ; and yet the
statute book of the kingdom in which this severity
originates, shall contain no warrant for executing
it, nor a syllable to soothe the anguish which it
has inflicted! Is it thus that God deals with his
people ? Does this look like his wonted conde-
scension to their infirmities ? Does it bear the
character of that loving kindness and tender
mercy which belong to him who " knows their
frame, and remembers that they are dust ?"

When the economy of Moses was to be super-
seded by that of Jesus Christ, he prepared the way
in the most gradual and gentle manner ; he showed
them from their own scriptures, that he had done

only what he had intended and predicted from the beginning; he set before their eyes a comparative view of the two dispensations, to satisfy them that they had lost nothing, but had gained much by the exchange. When they were "dull of hearing," he bore with their slowness; when they were extremely unwilling to part with Moses, he stooped to their infirmities; and persevered in his lenity, till the destruction of their city, their sacrifices, their temple, their nation, left their further demurring without the shadow of an excuse. But when he touched them in the point of most exquisite sensibility—when he passed a sword through their souls by cutting off their children, unable to distinguish between good and evil, from all the interest which they once had in his church, the heavy mandate is preceded by no warning, is accompanied with no comfort; is followed by nothing to replace the privation; is not even supported by a single reason! The thing is done in the most summary manner, and the order is not so much as entered into the rule of faith! The believing mother hears that the "son of her womb" is shut out from the covenant of her God, but hears not why! Is this the ordinance of him who, "as a father pitieth his children, so pities them that fear him?" It cannot be!

Conceding, then, to the opposers of our children's claim as members of the Christian church, all that they ask with regard to the *silence* of the New Testament, that very concession works their ruin. If their views are correct, it could not have been thus silent. Out of their own mouths we draw their conviction; and cast them in the judgment by the very evidence which they offer in their vindication.

The case is now reversed. Instead of *our* producing from the New Testament such a warrant for the privileges of our infant seed, as they require, we turn the tables upon them; and insist, that *they* shall produce scriptural proof of God's having *annulled the constitution under which we assert our right.* Till they do this, our cause is invincible. He once granted to his church the right for which we contend; and nothing but his own act can take it away. We want to *see the act of abrogation;* we must see it in the *New Testament;* for there it is, if it is at all. Point it out, and we have done. Till then we shall rejoice in the consolation of calling upon God as our God, and the God of our seed.

2. We have before remarked, that the exclusion of infants from the church of God, contradicts all the analogies of his external dispensations towards men.*

A correct reasoner will require the highest evidence of which the case is susceptible, before he

* Christian Magazine, Vol. I. p. 58—61.

admits a doctrine involving such a consequence. *General principles* are the great landmarks of truth. They furnish tests by which to try the soundness of those endless prepositions which are generated by the ceaseless activity of the human mind. *One* of them, well understood and judiciously applied, is a better preservative from errour, than a million of those small arguments by which multitudes regulate their opinion and their conduct.

If, indeed, it is the will of God that children shall not be esteemed, during their infancy, as members of the New Testament church; and if he has promulged his will in this matter by any explicit statute, or by any act which necessarily infers such an appointment, there is an end to all our difficulties and disquisitions. " Thus saith Jehovah," discharges, at once, every human inquiry. But seeing that, in every public constitution, he always identified parents with their children; and that in every other department of his government this principle is conspicuous at the present hour, an argument of the most imperious sort thence arises in favour of our children's birthright as members of his church. For as his constitutions of nature and of grace agree with the most wonderful harmony; and as this agreement is the foundation of all those references to the former, by which the scriptures explain and illustrate the latter, it is " passing strange," that he should

introduce, into the heart of his church, a law
which is at complete variance with the whole system of his creation and providence! that he should
go out of his way to make an exception, not *for*,
but *against*, his own people: refusing to them, as
members of his church, the benefit of an ordinance which in other societies erected by his authority, he freely allows to mankind at large; and
refusing it at the expense of resuming, without an
equivalent, the grant which he formerly conveyed
to them!

The case is still stronger when we reflect that
the children of believing parents participate in all
the *disasters* of the external church. If she be corrupted, the corruption infects them; if she be persecuted, the persecution smites them; if her mercies be sinned away, the punishment of the sin
lights on them. Could they suffer more upon the
supposition of their being really members? It
seems, then, that they are to share in all her af-
flictions, without sharing in her privileges: that
when evil overtakes her, they are to be treated as
citizens; but when her immunities are dispensed,
as aliens. So that the Lord our God *suspends* a
leading principle of his physical and moral order,
for the sake of barring the seed of his people from
privilege; and permits it to take its full course for
the infliction of *calamity!* This is more than incredible!

3. If the children of believing parents are not members of the church, before making a profession of their own faith, it follows, that from the day of their birth to the day of their conversion, they stand in no nearer relation to her than Pagans or Jews. A right to instruct, to warn, to entreat them, she certainly has; and she has the same right with regard to the Jew or the Pagan; but no *authority* over any of them. Her jurisdiction being necessarily confined to her own subjects; having no power to "judge them that are without;" and the children of her members being " without," she can take no cognizance of them which she might not take of infant or adult heathen who are within her reach. As it is their own act upon which they are admitted into her number, so it is that same act by which she acquires any right of directing them. Their parents she can enjoin to " bring them up in the nurture and admonition of the Lord," because God has rendered it a branch of parental duty; and she ought to enforce the observance of his law by all those spiritual means which he has confided to her zeal. But if parents be incapable of fulfilling their obligations; if they should happen to be separated from their families; to fail through negligence, or be cut off by death: or if the children prove refractory to parental admonition; in none of these cases can the church of God interpose any fur-

ther than to perform an act of voluntary benevo-
lence. *Authority* is out of the question. For what
authority can she have over those who never
sought her fellowship; to whom she has denied
her privileges; and whom she disowns as members? The same principle upon which she attempts to control the children of her members,
would justify her in attempting to legislate for
others who are without her pale, extending her discipline to Jews, Turks, Pagans; nay, to the whole
world lying in wickedness. If she may not do this,
the reason, and the only reason, is that they are
not her members; which reason is equally valid
in the case of children who are not her members.
The alternative is plain; either the church of God
must give up her care over youth who have not
made a profession of their faith; or in order to
exercise it must commit an act of usurpation.

But how can a Christian be reconciled to either
part of the alternative? How can he persuade
himself that children born of the people of God,
consecrated to his fear, and declared by his inspired apostle to be " holy," are no more members of his church, than the savage who wanders
upon the banks of the Missouri? How can he
persuade himself, that among the solemn trusts of
the Christian church, that most important one of
superintending the youth, has been omitted?
That she has received no charge, possesses no

power, and is under no responsibility, on this subject, further than to stimulate the individual efforts
of parents, masters, or teachers? If she has received any other commandment; if, in her *social*
character, she is bound to provide for " training
up a child in the way in which he should go,"
then the children to be so trained, must be treated as her members; and are members in fact, for
God never vested her with authority over any
who are not.

To set this point in another light. God, in the
ordinary course of his providence, does actually
gather his " true worshippers" from the families
of his people; and, for the most part, in the days
of their youth. He does it most conspicuously in
those churches which subject them, when young,
to the most exemplary inspection. He has, on
the other hand, frowned upon churches as they
became remiss in this particular; his good Spirit
has departed from them; and there are not a few
which, at this hour, may trace their declension
and the rapid approach of their desolation, to the
neglect of their youth. But to deny that children
are members of the church, is to deny both her
duty and her right to exercise any public authority over them; and to deny it in opposition both
to the blessing and the curse of God; is to smite
the Redeemer's kingdom in the heart of one of
its most precious interests, the youth; and to do

it much deeper and more effectual injury, than it is likely to suffer from the assaults of open enemies.

These consequences appear to us inevitable. Far from us be the thought of imputing them to those who reject the church membership of infants; or of asserting that they do in fact occur as regularly as we might expect. For, on the one hand, God does not permit Errour to mature all the deadly fruits which she is capable of bearing : and, on the other, the nature of human society is not to be subverted by theory. Let men profess what they please; let them renounce, and if they think fit, ridicule, our doctrine; it is nevertheless true, that they cannot get along in the religious any more than in the civil community, without more or less considering children as members. And it is their acting upon the very principle which they represent as unscriptural and absurd, that saves their churches from speedy destruction.

4. From the date of the covenant with Abraham, to the cessation of the Mosaic law, infants were undoubtedly members of God's church The seal of his covenant was in their flesh ; and it was deemed by every Hebrew a prerogative of inestimable worth. " Uncircumcised," was the most bitter and disdainful reproach which his mouth could utter. He would sooner lay his sons in the grave, than permit them go without

the token of their being Abraham's seed. On these facts we found three inquiries. The first relating to the privilege which God conferred upon his people; the second to the effect which the recalling of it produced on them; and the third to their state of feeling under the loss.

First. " The sign of circumcision, a seal of the righteousness of faith," applied, by divine direction, to infant members of the church, was a high privilege.

This cannot, with even a show of reason, be disputed. That God should subject them to a painful rite which was of no use—that the indelible certification of his being their God as he had been the God of their fathers, should be coupled with no benefit—that he should draw them into covenant relations which were good for nothing, no man is sottish enough to pretend. Their condition, therefore, as members of his church, and the sacramental sign of it, was a real and an important privilege.

What has become of it ?

If infants are no longer members of his church, it is taken away, and what has replaced it ? Nothing, Nothing ! then God has put the children of his people under the new dispensation, further from him than they were under the old. He has inverted his method of providence toward his church, which has uniformly been to bless her

with *progressive* light and favour.   The communication of his grace and truth always increasing,
never diminished. Each succeeding dispensation
comprehending the whole mass of benefits which
belonged to the preceding, and adding others of
its own.   But in this solitary, instance the course
of his covenant is changed ! And whereas he had
formerly separated his people from the heathen
that knew him not; had drawn around them a
line of covenant goodness; had put their *little ones*
within the holy circle ; and had instructed them
to cherish the distinction as, in his sight, of great
price—yet now, when he is to enlarge their inheritance, and enrich their joys ; to fulfil the promise of those good things which " eye had not
seen, nor ear heard, neither had entered into the
heart of man," he *begins* with telling them that
though he will still be *their* God, he will no longer
be the God of their *seed ;* that he has cast their
babes out of his church, over the line of his covenant, in among the " dogs." And all this, after
he had sworn that he would " not break his covenant, nor alter the thing that had gone out of his
mouth :" and having done it, commissions his
apostle to declare, that " his gifts and his calling
are without repentance ;" i. e. that a grant which
he has once made to his church, he never annuls !
Believe it who can.*

* Rom. xi. 29. That the unchangeableness of God's gifts and

Let us, however, allow that we have miscon-
strued the divine covenant; and that infants born
after the settlement of the new economy, had no
such claim as had the infant posterity of Abraham. How did the arrangement affect the children of those who were the first members of the
Christian church? For example, those who were
added to her on the day of Pentecost? This is our
Second Inquiry.

The rule of God's proceeding against those
who should reject the Messiah, was laid down by
Moses; and is thus quoted and explained by the
apostle Peter : " *Moses truly said unto the Fathers,
a prophet shall the Lord your God raise up unto you,
of your brethren, like unto me; him shall ye hear in all
things whatsoever he shall say unto you. And it shall
come to pass, that* EVERY SOUL WHICH WILL NOT HEAR
THAT PROPHET, SHALL BE DESTROYED FROM AMONG
THE PEOPLE. Act. iii. 22, 23. ··

calling refers to his church, we conclude from the whole scope of
the apostle's reasoning in the context; part of which proves the
recovery of Israel to the mercies of their fathers; and proves it
from the consideration, that it is God's gracious design to rein-
state them in their privileges ; that this design is to be accomplished in virtue of the " gifts and calling" to their fathers Abraham,
Isaac, and Jacob. And as they cannot be reinstated but by embracing Christianity, these unchangeable "gifts and calling," must
be continued in the New Testament church. Infant membership
was, incontrovertibly, one of the gifts: therefore, if the children
of his people are not members of his church, God *has* broken his
covenant.

The sin of which the Jews were warned by their great law-giver, was their not obeying the voice of his great successor; that is, the sin of rejecting the Messiah. The punishment denounced against this sin, was " *destruction from among the* PEOPLE." Who were the people ? And what was the destruction ?

(1.) Who were the *people?*

Not the *nation* of the Jews. For, having committed the crime, they themselves fell under the penalty. Their nation was to be destroyed; whereas, according to the prediction of Moses, it was not the *people* that were to perish ; but the *disobedient* who were to be destroyed from *among* the people; which implies the continuance of that people in the divine protection. It is a people, therefore, which was to survive the rejection of the Jews, and be placed in such circumstances of favour, as to render destruction from among them a great and terrible judgment.

Not the people whom God " hath chosen in Christ before the foundation of the world, that they should be holy." For God never *cast away his people whom he foreknew.** They who committed the crime before us, never belonged to his people, and so could not be destroyed from among them ; and they whom God had thus chosen did

* Rom. xi. 2.   Acts xiii. 48.

not commit the crime. " *As many as were ordained unto eternal life,* BELIEVED."

Who then are " the people" from among whom
the sinners were to be destroyed? If not the
Jewish people, if not the *elected* people of God, it
can be no other than that PEOPLE whom he
owns as his, and who are called by the collective
name of his CHURCH.*

(2.) What was the " destruction ?"

Not temporal death : for God never ordained
this punishment for the sin of unbelief on his son.

Not an exclusion from the communion of the
Jewish nation; for unbelief in Christ was to them
a recommendation instead of a disparagement;
and to be severed from them entirely, was at least
as likely to prove a blessing as a curse.

In what, then, did the destruction consist? Un-

---

* This passage furnishes an irrefragable proof of the unity and
perpetuity of the *Visible Church.*

For, 1. These rebels were a *part* of the people from among
whom they were to be destroyed : which people we have proved,
could be no other than the people or church of God.

2. The people or church from which they were to be destroyed,
was to remain a people, and the peculiar object of the divine regard. This is true of no people but that which composes his
church. The Christian chuch is therefore the *very same* church
from which the Jews were cast out.

3. The term "people" cannot designate the church otherwise
than as a *great* WHOLE. The more we " search the scriptures,"
the more does a "cloud of witnesses" thicken round us to testify
that " the Church of God is ONE."

doubtedly, in having their name and place exterminated from among the people of God; in being cast out of his church, and exposed to that perdition which shall be the fate of all whom he disowns. This must be the interpretation of the threatening, because no other will comport with either sense or fact.

Let us now see how this bears upon the point before us.

The unbelieving Jews were cut off, for their unbelief, from the church of God; and, surely, it will not be accounted the least part of the vengeance, that their children shared their fate.

But the case of believing Jews was exactly the reverse. If they who would not hear the divine prophet were to be destroyed from among the people; it certainly follows, that they who would and did hear him, should not be destroyed; but should retain their place and privileges. And if, in the execution of the curse upon the disobedient, their children also were cut off; then, God's own act establishing the principle of judgment, the children of those who were not disobedient, participated in their blessing; i. e. instead of being destroyed from among the people, were numbered with them; or, which is the same, were, by his own authority, reckoned members of his church.

These infants, then, being in the church of God

already, the question is, by what authority were
they cast out? It would be an unheard of thing if
the faith of their parents in the " consolation of
Israel," should expel them. A singular way, indeed, of converting a Jew, to tell him that the
very fact of his being a believer in Christ would
excommunicate his children! The issue is short.
Either the children of believing Jews were members of the church under her Christian form, or
not. If not, then, in so far as their children were
concerned, God inflicted upon the *faith* of parents,
that very curse which he had threatened upon
their *unbelief.* If otherwise, then at the very beginning of the new dispensation, infants were
members of his church. We give our opponents,
their option.

We have yet to answer a

Third Inquiry, concerning the excision of infants from the New Testament church: or, if you
prefer it, their non-admission to her privileges.

How must such a measure have operated upon
the feelings of a believing Jew?

Tenacious, in a high degree, of their peculiarities—regarding their relation to Abraham as
momentous to their individual happiness; and as
the most prominent feature of their national glory
—knowing, too, that their children were comprised with themselves in the covenant of God, it is
not possible that the Hebrews could have sub-

mitted, without reluctance, to a constitution which
was to strip them of their favourite privilege; to
dissever their tenderest ties; to blot the names of
their little ones out of the register of God's people; and treat them afterwards, from generation
to generation, as the little ones of the heathen
man and the publican ! On every other prerogative, real or imaginary, their suspicion was awake,
their zeal inflammable, their passions intractable.
But toward this, their grand prerogative, they
evinced a tameness which required them to forget, at once, that they were men and that they
were Jews.   Search the records of the New Testament from one end to the other, and you will
not find the trace of a remonstrance, an objection, or a difficulty on this subject, from the mouth
of either a believing or an unbelieving Israelite !
The former never parted with a tittle of even the
Mosaic law, till the will of God was so clearly
demonstrated as to remove every doubt : the latter lay constantly in wait for matter of accusation
against the Christians.   Nothing could have
prompted him to louder clamour, to fiercer resistance, or to heavier charges, than an attempt to
overturn a fundamental principle of the covenant
with Abraham : nothing could have more startled
and distressed the meek and modest disciple.
Yet that attempt is made; that fundamental principle of the covenant with Abraham, is overturn-

ed; and not a friend complains, nor a foe resents! What miracle of enchantment has so instantaneously relieved the conscience of the one, and calmed the warmth of the other? Where is that wayward vanity, that captious criticism, that combustible temperament, that insidious, implacable, restless enmity, which by night and by day, in country and in town, haunted the steps of the apostles, and treasured up actions, words, looks, for the hour of convenient vengeance? All gone; dissipated in a moment! The proud and persecuting Pharisee rages at the name of Jesus Christ; fights for his traditions and his phylacteries; and utters not a syllable of dissent from a step which completely annihilates the covenant with Abraham! that very covenant from which he professes to derive his whole importance!! We can believe a great deal, but not quite so much as this.

Should it be alleged, that the Jews did probably oppose the exclusion of their infants from the New Testament church, although the sacred writers have omitted to mention it: we reply,

That although many things have happened which were never recorded; and, therefore, that the mere silence of an historian, is not, in itself, conclusive against their existence; yet no man may assume, as proof, the existence of a fact which is unsupported by either history or tradition. On this ground, the plea which we have stopped to notice is perfectly nugatory.

In the present case, however, the probabilities look all the other way. We mean, that if the Jews had made the opposition, which on the supposition we are combatting, it is inconceivable they should not have made, it would have been so interwoven with the origin, constitution, progress, and transactions of the primitive church, as to have rendered an omission of it almost impossible.

The question about circumcision and the obligation on the Gentile converts to keep the law of Moses, shook the churches to their centre; and was not put at rest but by a formal decision of the apostles and elders. Now as circumcision was the seal of the Abrahamic covenant, which explicitly constituted infants members of the church, is it to be imagined that so hot a controversy should have been kindled about the ensealing rite, and none at all about the privilege sealed? or that a record should have been carefully preserved of the disputes and decision concerning the *sign;* and no record at all kept of the discussions concerning the *thing signified,* which imparted to the former all their interest and value?

It is, therefore, utterly incredible that the resistance of Jews to the Christian arrangement for shutting out their children from the church of God, should have passed unnoticed. But no notice of any such resistance is in the New Testament. The conclusion is, that no such resistance was ever offered : and the conclusion from this again is, that no cause for it existed; that is, that the infants of professing parents were considered as holding, under the new economy, the same place and relation which they held under the old.

Our conclusion acquires much force from the nature of the controversy respecting circumcision. The Judaizing teachers made the observance of this rite, a term, not only of communion, but of salvation. *Except ye be circumcised,* said they, *and keep the law of Moses, ye cannot he saved.* Had their doctrine prevailed, circumcision in the Christian church must have been regulated by the Mosaic law. But this law prescribed the circumcision of infants. Now, under what pretext could they urge a compliance with this ordinance, according to the law of Moses, upon the Gentile converts, unless it were *an undisputed point* that the children of these converts were members of the Christian church ? An exception was at hand. " Whatever may be the duty of *adults,* there is no reason to circumcise *infants ;* because, by the new order of things, they do not belong to the Christian community, and have no concern with its sealing ordinances." Yet no such exception was ever taken.

This one fact, under all its circumstances and connexions,* is equivalent to a doctrinal declaration of the apostles and elders at Jerusalem, that the change of dispensation has not affected the rights of infants born of believing parents; and that they are under the Christian, as really as they were under the Mosaic, economy, members of the church of God; and as fully entitled to its initiating ordinance.

5. The *language* of God's word, respecting children, is in perfect accordance with the principle of their being members of his church; but is irreconcileable with the contrary supposition.

Enumerating some of the benefits of the new economy, he says, by the prophet Isaiah, that his people " shall not labour in vain, nor bring forth for " trouble; for they are the seed of the blessed of the Lord, and their *offspring with them.*"† The Redeemer, in the days of his flesh, was much displeased with an attempt of his disciples to keep back infants from approaching him, and said, " Suffer the little children to come unto me, and forbid them not, for *of such is the kingdon of God.*"‡ An expression which, we well know, signifies the New Testament church. " The promise," said Peter, after the descent of the Holy Spirit at Pentecost, " The promise is to you, and to *your children.*"§

* Compare Acts xxi. 21.   ‡ Mark x. 14.
† Is. lxv. 23.   § Acts ii. 39.

These and similar expressions, with which the word of God abounds, correspond much better to that system which associates children with their parents in his church, than with that which rejects them as no part of it. And we must have very strong reasons to justify our embracing a system which requires a language contrary to the genius of the language which the Holy Spirit himself has selected.

6. Unless we greatly mistake, the apostle Paul has twice decided the question before us in the most unequivocal manner; and decided it in our favour.

One of his decisions is in the following words: " The unbelieving husband is sanctified by the wife; and the unbelieving wife is sanctified by the husband; *else were your children* UNCLEAN, *but now are they* HOLY."*

In what sense does a believing, sanctify an unbelieving, parent, so that their *children* are holy? Wherein does this holiness consist? Some have been so galled by this assertion of the apostle, that they have tried to fritter it down into a grave declaration of the legitimacy of children born of parents thus situated. As if faith in Christ were necessary to the validity of espousals ! As if all the marriages of the heathen were mere concubi-

* 1 Cor. vii. 14.

nage; and all their children the fruit of illicit amours!

The apostle certainly does not mean that one parent communicates to another, or that either of them communicates to their children, that internal conformity to the divine purity, which is commonly called " holiness" or santification. This is contrary to reason, to scripture, and to daily experience. Yet he says that a believing parent renders holy the unbelieving one; and that, in consequence, their children are holy. What does he mean?

" Holy," as a term of established use and signification, was well understood by the Corinthian Christians. It expresses the state of a person or thing specially separated to the service of God; and in which, by reason of that separation, he acquires a peculiar property. For this interpretation we have his own authority—when prohibiting various pollutions, he thus addresses the people of Israel; *Ye shall be* HOLY *unto me : for I the Lord am holy ; and* HAVE SEVERED *you from other people, that ye should be* MINE. Lev. xx. 26. This " severing" was effected by his covenant with them. They were " holy," because they belonged to his church, which he had erected to put his name and his glory there.

" Unclean," as contrasted with " holy," express es the state of a person not separated to the service of God : in whom he has no peculiar interest, and who is, therefore, " common ;" i. e. *unappropriated to God.* All who are conversant with the scriptural phraseology know this representation to be true.

What, then, does the apostle say ? He says that if the unbelieving, were *not* sanctified by the believing, parent, their children would be "unclean ;" would be " common ;" would have no peculiar relation to God, nor any place in his church. But since the believing, *does* sanctify the unbelieving, parent, their children are the reverse of "unclean :" they are " holy ;" they are born under peculiar relations to God ; they are appropriated to him ; they are members of his church ; and as they undoubtedly have a right to the token of their membership—to baptism.

Considering the nature of the scriptural style ; and that " holy," and " unclean," or " common," are the precise terms for such as were, and as were not, respectively, within the external covenant of God, we are unable to conceive how the apostle could more formally and unequivocally have declared the church membership of infants born of a believing parent. The first of these terms was, in his mouth, exactly what " a member of the church" is in ours ; and could not be otherwise understood by the primitive Christians.

The only plausible difficulty which lies against
our view, is, that "According to the same
reasoning, an unbeliever, *continuing in unbelief*, becomes a member of the church in consequence of
marriage with a believer. For the apostle does
not more positively affirm that the children are
" holy," than he affirms that the unbelieving husband is sanctified by the wife, and the unbelieving
wife sanctified, or " made holy," by the husband.
Therefore, if holiness imparted by the parent to
the children, makes them members of the church,
the holiness imparted by one parent to the other,
makes him or her, a member of the church. This
will not be maintained. For it would be absurd
to imagine, that an infidel adult, living in open
hostility to the church of God, should be reckoned among its members merely in virtue of union
to a believing husband or wife. Well then, if the
" sanctification," which an unbelieving wife derives from her believing husband, does not make
her a member of the church, the "holiness" which
children derive from a believing parent, cannot
make *them* members of the church."

The objection is shrewd : but, like many other
shrewd things, more calculated to embarrass
an inquirer, than to assist him. Our answer is
short.

First, It makes the apostle talk nonsense. The
amount of it when stripped of its speciousness

and tried by the standard of common sense, being neither more nor less than this, that all his discourse about the sanctification of husband and wife, and the holiness of their children, means— just *nothing at all.* For if it be not an internal holiness, which we do not affirm ; nor an external relative holiness, which the objection denies; then a person is said by the apostle to be holy, whose holiness is neither within him nor without him ; neither in soul, nor spirit, nor body, nor state, nor condition, nor any thing else: which, in our apprehension, is as genuine nonsense as can well be uttered. If those who differ from us feel themselves wronged, we beg them to show *in what the holiness mentioned by the apostle consists.*

Secondly. The objection takes for granted, that the sanctification of the husband by his wife, or of the wife by her husband, is precisely of the same *extent,* and produces on its subject the same *effect,* as the holiness which children inherit from a believing parent. This is certainly erroneous.

(1.) The covenant of God never founded the privilege of membership in his church upon the mere fact of *intermarriage* with his people : but it did expressly found that privilege upon the fact of being *born* of them.

(2.) By a positive precept, adults were not to be admitted into the church without a profession of their faith. This is a special statute, limiting, in the case of adults, the general doctrine of membership. Consequently, the doctrine of Paul must be explained by the restriction of that statute. " Sanctify" her unbelieving husband the believing wife does ; and so does the believing husband his unbelieving wife; i. e. to a *certain length ;* but not *so far* as to render the partner thus sanctified, a member of the church—The former cannot be doubted, for the apostle peremptorily asserts it—The latter cannot be admitted ; for it would contravene the statute already quoted. The membership of infants does not contravene it. And, therefore, although the holiness which the apostle ascribes to infants involves *their* membership ; it does not follow that the sanctifying influence over an unbelieving husband or wife, which he ascribes to the believing wife or husband, involves the church membership of the party thus sanctified.

(3.) The very words of the text lead to the same conclusion. They teach us, in the plainest manner, that this sanctification regards the unbelieving parent not *for his own sake,* but as a *medium* affecting the transmission of covenant privilege to the *children of a believer.*

A simple, and we think, satisfactory account of the matter, is this :

Among the early conversions to Christianity, it often happened, that the gospel was believed by a woman, and rejected by her husband; or believed by a man, and rejected by his wife. One of the invariable effects of Christianity being a tender concern in parents for the welfare of their off-spring ; a question was naturally suggested by such a disparity of religious condition, as to the light in which the children were to be viewed. Considering the one parent, they were to be accounted " holy ;" but considering the other, they were to be accounted " unclean." Did the character of the former place them *within* the church of God; or the character of the latter *without* it ? or did they belong partly to the church and partly to the world, but wholly to neither? The difficulty was a real one ; and calculated to excite much distress in the minds of parents who, like the primitive Christians, did not treat the relation of their little ones to the church of God, as a slight and uninteresting affair.

Paul obviates it by telling his Corinthian friends, that in this case where the argument *for* the children appears to be perfectly balanced by the argument *against* them, God has graciously inclined the scale in *favour* of his people : so that *for the purpose of conveying to their infants the privilege of being within his covenant and church*, the unbelieving husband is sanctified by the wife, and the unbelieving wife by the husband. If it were not so, it must be the reverse ; because it is impossible that

a child should be born in *two* contrary moral
states : *then*, the believing husband being rendered " unclean" by his wife ; and the believing wife
" unclean" by her husband, their children would
also be " unclean," i. e. would be born, not in a
state of separation *to* God; but in a state of separation *from* him ; like those who are without the
bond of his covenant, and, not being *appropriated*
to him, are " common" or " unclean." But now,
saith the apostle, God has determined that the
parental influence shall go the other way. That
instead of the interest which a child has in his
covenant, by virtue of the faith of one parent,
being made void by the infidelity of the other ;
the very fact of being married to a believer, shall
so far *control* the effect of unbelief—shall so far
consecrate the infidel party, as that the children of
such a marriage shall be accounted of the covenanted seed ; shall be members of the church—
Now, saith Paul, *they are* HOLY.

The passage which we have explained, establishes the church membership of infants in another form. For it assumes the principle that when
both parents are reputed believers, their children
belong to the church of God as *a matter of course.*
The whole difficulty proposed by the Corinthians
to Paul grows out of this principle. Had he
taught, or they understood, that *no* children, be
their parents believers or unbelievers, are to be

accounted members of the church, the difficulty could not have existed. For if the faith of *both* parents could not confer upon a child the privilege of membership, the faith of only *one* of them certainly could not. The point was decided. It would have been mere impertinence to teaze the apostle with queries which carried their own answer along with them. But on the supposition that when both parents were members, their children, also, were members; the difficulty is very natural and serious. " I see," would a Corinthian convert exclaim, " I see the children of my Christian neighbours, owned as members of the church of God; and I see the children of others, who are unbelievers, rejected with themselves. I believe in Christ myself; but my husband, my wife, believes not. " What is to become of *my* children? Are they to be admitted with myself? or are they to be cast off with my partner ?"

" Let not your heart be troubled," replies the apostle : " God reckons them to the believing, not to the unbelieving, parent. It is enough that they are *yours*. The infidelity of your partner shall never frustrate their interest in the covenant of your God. They are 'holy' because you are so."

This decision put the subject at rest. And it lets us know that one of the reasons, if not the chief reason of the doubt, whether a married person should continue, after conversion, in the conjugal society of an infidel partner, arose from a fear lest such continuance should exclude the children from the church of God. Otherwise it is hard to comprehend why the apostle should dissuade them from separating, by such an argument as he has employed in the text. And it is utterly inconceivable how such a doubt could have entered their minds, had not the membership of infants, born of believing parents, been undisputed, and esteemed a high privilege; *so* high a privilege, as that the apprehension of losing it made conscientious parents at a stand whether they ought not rather to break the ties of wedlock, by withdrawing from an unbelieving husband or wife. Thus, the *origin* of this difficulty on the one hand, and the *solution* of it, on the other, concur in establishing our doctrine, that, by the appointment of God himself, the *infants of believing parents are* BORN *members of his church.*

We shall close this number, already too long, though but an outline, with another decision on the same general question, from the pen of the same apostle.

Treating of the future restoration of the Jews, he says, *They also, if they bide not still in unbelief, shall be* GRAFFED *in; for God is able to graff them in* AGAIN. *For if thou wert cut out of the olive tree which is wild by nature; and wert graffed, contrary to nature, into a good olive tree; how much more shall*

these, which be the natural branches, *be graffed into
their* OWN OLIVE TREE. Rom. xi. 23, 24.

That the olive tree signifies, and *can* signify nothing else than the *visible church* with the privileges dispensed in it, we abundantly proved in our
second number.* The Jews never did belong,
nationally, to any but the external church; and
from no other could they be cut off. But, saith
Paul, these Jews, "the natural branches," have
been "broken off," and thou the Gentile, "graffed
in." Graffed into what? The *same* tree from
which the others were cut away. Then, not only
is there a *visible church;* but it is the *very same*
from which the Jews have been excommunicated.
Or else the apostle has asserted a falsehood. For
if the New Testament church be not the same,
in substance, with the church to which the Jews
belonged, it is not true that the Gentiles have
been "graffed into the olive tree," from which the
Jews have been broken off; but a *new tree* has
been planted: a flat and formal.contradiction to
the word of God! which says, that the *old tree
stands,* and that other *branches* are graffed in.
Well, then, the Gentiles occupy in the church the
place which the Jews did before their expulsion.
The new branch with *its buds* is transferred to the
good olive tree, and grows in its fatness. Whatever privileges, therefore, the Jews had formerly,

45—47.

as *members of the church of God*, all these, at least,
their Gentile successors enjoy.   But the membership of their infants was one of these privileges;
a principle one.   Therefore, the children of Gentile believers are members of the Christian church.

Turn, now, the argument.   The Jews are to be
restored.   These, the " natural branches," shall
be " graffed in again"—shall be " graffed into their
own olive tree."   AGAIN! Into their OWN olive
tree! Then *their own* tree is preserved.   But
mark, the Gentile branches are not to be cut off.
So then, the Jews and Gentiles will belong to *one*
church; will be branches of the *same* olive tree.
But they are to be graffed into their *own* tree,
says Paul.   The consequence returns irresistibly
upon us.   The church of God under both dispensations is *one and the same.*   Or else the apostle
has told another falsehood.   For if it be not the
same, as the Jews are to come into the Christian
church, they will not be graffed into their *own*
olive tree, but into another.

But the Jews, before their excision, were with
their children, members of the church.   If, then,
they be *reinstated;* or as the apostle expresses it,
graffed in *again*, their children also must be members of the church, or else God will break his promise, and the Holy Spirit of truth, deceive their
hope.   The restored Jews, however, can derive
their privileges only through the medium of the

New Testament church. The membership of their infants is one of the privileges to be so derived; therefore, the *infants of believing parents are members of the New Testament church.*—Which was to be demonstrated.

CHURCH OF GOD.

No. VI.

Uses.

BELIEVING that the preceding numbers contain a true and scriptural account of the visible church in general, we think it proper, before inquiring into its particular provisions, to point out some of the ends which it is calculated to answer, and some of the consequences which result from our doctrine.

Let us briefly recapitulate.

Adults who make a credible profession of their faith, are to be admitted as members.*

Children of believing parents, that is, of visible Christians, are members in virtue of their birth.†

So that the Catholic church consists of all them who, throughout the world, profess the true religion; and of their children.

This great community, which is but one, has

* What a credible profession is, see No. III. p. 48—58.
† For the proof of this, see our last No. p. 85—121.

special external covenant relations to the Most
High God; the fundamental principle of which is,
a dispensation of grace through a Redeemer; and,
as an effect of these relations, enjoys special privileges in which her members have a right to participate according to their circumstances.

From the very nature of the case, it must and
does happen, that many of these members are
Christians only in name : such as never have
been, and never shall be, vitally united to Christ,
but shall die in their iniquity. Yet if their un-
soundness be not detected ; if by no outward
act they reproach that worthy name by which
they are called, their right, even to sacramental
privilege, is as firm and full as the right of a believer who shall hold the highest place among the
saved. The reason, which has been illustrated
already, is, that Christian ordinances are administered by men ; and the secret state of the soul
before God is not, and cannot be, their rule of
judgment. In this case, appearances and realities
are, to them, the same; because they have no
means of forming an opinion of realities but from
appearances : and, therefore, officers in the house
of God may, with the most perfect good conscience and fidelity, give the seals of his covenant
to such as shall turn out to be sons and daughters of perdition. If it were not so, not one
among all the ministers of the gospel since the

ascension of our Lord Jesus, could escape being arraigned for treason at his bar. For not one of them would dare to affirm, that he had not, in a single instance, given the sacramental sign to an unbeliever.

Seeing, then, that false professors and true; the sincere and the hypocritical; elected men and reprobates, are mingled together in the external church; and that there are no human means of separating the " chaff which shall be burnt up with unquenchable fire," from the " wheat which shall be gathered into the garner" of God, what purpose does such a constitution serve? Does not the idea that such a strange commixture should be a church of God shock the mind? Is it not unfriendly to piety? And would it not be much better if saints alone were to be admitted within her pale, to the utter and absolute exclusion of hypocrites and reprobates?

Doubtless many think so. For men are apt to conceit that they can mend the works of God. And such multitudes of expriments have been made, in this way, upon his church, that if he had not been her keeper she would have perished ages ago. When he shall employ us to set up a church, it will be soon enough to display our skill, In the mean time, let us thankfully submit to his appointments; and humbly inquire whether we cannot discover in that very constitution which has been described, something not unworthy of his wisdom and his goodness too.

There is a strong analogy between the kingdom of heaven in the *heart*, in the *world*, and in the *church*. Not one of them is free from evil : nor is designed to be so in the present state. The *world* teems with sin ; it is full of plagues and curses : but it is still *God's* world ; the subject of his government, and the theatre of his grace. The renewed heart is infested with depravity. Sin dwells in them who bear most of their Saviour's image, enjoy the largest share of his communion, and approach the nearest to his perfection. *If we say that we have no sin, we deceive ourselves, and the truth is not in us.** But this " sin that dwelleth in them," does not hinder them from being in soul and body, *the temples of the Holy Ghost.*† It would be quite as reasonable to maintain, that a Christian cannot be a child of God because there *is a law in his members warring against the law of his mind :*‡ or that the world is not God's world because *the tumult of those that rise up against him increaseth continually ;*‖ as to maintain that a church composed partly of converts and partly of the unconverted, is not for that reason, a true nor a scriptural church. The neighbourhood and conflict of good and evil in this life is

* 1 John i. 8.   ‡ Rom. vii. 23.
† 1 Cor. vi. 19.   ‖ Ps. lxxiv. 23.

one of those depths which nothing but folly attempts to fathom; yet while the mystery is unsearchable, the doctrine is clear, and the fact notorious. Whoever, then, shall deny that God has so constituted his church here as to include concealed enemies in the midst of real friends; and has left no method of drawing, with certainty, the line of practical discrimination; must go further, and deny that he has so constituted his world as to admit the introduction of sin, and has left no method of expelling it: or has so constituted the plan of salvation, as to allow corrupt affections to reside in the hallowed breast, and has left no method of extirpating them. The objection is precisely the same in the three cases. He who can answer it in one, can answer it in all; and he who cannot answer it in all, can answer it in none.

On the other hand, whoever can find it consistent with the divine perfection, that wicked men should be in the world; and wicked propensities in the soul of a believer, and yet the world be acknowledged by God as his world, and the believer as his child; will find it equally consistent with his perfection that servants of sin as well as servants of righteousness should belong to the church, and yet she be owned of him as his church.

Nor will this reasoning operate, in the smallest degree, against her sacredness as holy to the Lord; nor impair our obligation to promote her purity; nor afford the slightest countenance to careless admission into her communion, or the relaxation of her discipline toward the scandalous. For although God will glorify himself by bringing good out of evil, it is damnable in *us* to " do evil that good may come."* And although he, in that sovereignty which " giveth no account of any of his matters," has permitted and overrules the sin of the creature for purposes worthy of himself; yet we are not seated in the throne of sovereignty; we are under law; and the law of our duty is plain, so that " he may run who readeth," that we are to *resist, even unto blood, striving against sin.*† It no more follows that his church is not to thrust from her embrace the known servants of sin, because her vigilance may be eluded and her efforts defeated; than it follows that believers may indulge themselves in the commission of sin, because all their exertions will be insufficient to destroy it while they are in the body; or than it follows, that crimes are to stalk unquestioned through the earth, because they cannot be entirely cut off. The more closely this analogy is pressed, the more exactly will it be found to hold. And hence arises the general reason why the church of God, according to our principles, is well and wisely constituted—It is precisely adapt-

* Rom. iii. 8.   † Heb. xii. 8.

ed to the state of our world, and to the course of his own dispensations.

The analogy which we have now pointed out might convince the intelligent Christian, and silence the modest one. To the former it offers a decisive character of truth; and the latter will ask no better argument for the goodness of a constitution, than it is a constitution of God. But we need not rest the matter here. Without prying into the reservations of his wisdom, we may perceive some valuable ends to be answered by the mixed state of his church.

1. It reduces the quantity of actual sin.

We cannot too deeply deplore the fact that many " have a name to live and are dead." They are numbered with the people of God. Their reputation among their fellow professors is pure. Yet they have not " passed from death unto life." A terrible condition, no doubt; and a preparation for a terrible doom. But let us consider what would be the effect if all those sins should be disclosed in this world which shall be disclosed when the " secrets of all hearts shall be made manifest." Or, if this be too strong; what would be the effect, should those corruptions which are not subdued by divine grace, be set free from the restraints supplied through the external church. Could you unmask the hypocrite, and throw him at once out of your fellowship, and confidence, all

the motives and influence which serve to curb his
lusts, and limit their mischief, would cease to
operate; and that fountain of iniquity which is
now shut up in darkness would break out into
open day, and pour its poisonous streams in every
direction. It is impossible to conjecture how far
the law of God's house, and liberal intercourse
with his people, frustrate the worst designs of hell
by *shackling* the depravity of its servants. Some,
perhaps, may contend that it were better to see
every bad man in his own colours, that we might
completely " purge out the old leaven." Their
zeal is not according to knowledge—They inad-
vertently reproach the wisdom of God, who does
not permit such a discovery to be made. And
what would they have? Would it be better that
an enemy to God should give scope to his enmity,
and spread infection and death all around him,
than that the repression of it should tie up his
hands, and render him comparatively harmless?
Would it be better that he should blaspheme the
name of God, than that he should treat it with
external reverence? Better, to set before his
children or companions an example of hideous
profligacy, than an example of decorum! to teach
them to swear, steal, lie, profane the sabbath,
deride their bible, mock the ordinances of religion, than to inculcate upon them lessons of truth,
of probity, of respect to the name, the day, the

word, and the worship of God! Go a step further,
and say that it would be better to lay aside all
the control of civil government, and let loose the
myriads of rogues and traitors whom the community unwittingly cherishes in her bosom, than
to keep them under the salutary awe of the tribunals of Justice, of the dungeon and the halter.

Besides, men who only profess religion, while
they are strangers to its power, have much more
extensive connexions with those who profess
none, than real Christians can or ought to have.
There is not that mutual repugnance which renders society reserved and suspicious; and thus
they become a medium of transmitting the *moral*
influence of the gospel to thousands and tens of
thousands who yield no intentional obedience to
its authority. Real Christians act directly upon
professed ones; and these, again, upon men who
make no profession at all; and thus, through an
infinite number of channels unnoticed and unknown, Christianity streams its influence over human Society; gives a tone to public opinion, and
a purity to public and individual manners, which
are derivable from no other source. The very
infidel is by this means instructed in all the truth
he knows. He has an impulse given to his faculties; a check to his passions; and a rein to his
actions, of which he is unconscious. But if you
could turn out of the church all who are not heirs

according to the promise of eternal life, you would, in a great measure, defeat the benign influence of the gospel upon the civil community ; because you would destroy many points of their contract, and remove thousands altogether from its sphere of action ; or, which is the same thing, contract the sphere so as to leave out thousands who are now within it.   Admitting, then, without scruple, the just cause of grief which is afforded by the Canaanite's being in the house of the Lord, we are consoled with observing how he brings good out of evil.   Satan thrusts himself and his accomplices into the assembly of the saints ; and God converts the intrusion into a chain for them both. Thus the visible church, composed of believers and hypocrites, effects, by this very principle, an incalculable diminution of the actual sin which would otherwise be in the world.

2. It diminishes the misery of human life.

This is a direct consequence of prevented sin. For in proportion as the laws of God are violated, is the aggregate suffering of the community increased : and in proportion as they are respected, is its character amiable, and its condition prosperous.   Who can doubt, even for a moment, that the abandonment of all nominal Christians to the unsanctified propensities of their nature, would multiply crimes and accelerate individual and public ruin ? And who can doubt, that the check im-

posed on these propensities by an outward profession of the cross of Christ, averts calamity
which would otherwise be both certain and se-
vere? Let us not overlook the immense difference
between temporal and eternal good; and between
the means by which they are respectively procured. The religion which will not save a soul
from hell, may yet save a nation from destruction.
It is only upon gross transgression, freely and ob-
stinately committed, that God inflicts those evils
which he calls " his judgments." There may be
much secret impiety; much smothered opposition
to his government, but it must break out; must
become flagrant; must resist the milder correc-
tives, before he " arise to shake terribly the earth."
It is for no small provocation that he " bathes his
sword in heaven;" nor is it easy for a people to
" fill their cup." He may visit; he may chastise;
always, however, for open sin. But the cry for
vengeance must be loud and long before he resign a land to desolation, and mark it so irrever-
sibly for his curse, that *though Noah, Daniel, and
Job were in it, they should deliver neither son nor
daughter;* but merely *their own souls by their righteousness;** and *though Moses and Samuel stood before him, his mind could not be toward it.*† We are
not unaccustomed to the clamour which some,
who know not what they say, nor whereof they affirm,

* Ezek. xiv. † Jerem. xv.

and yet *desire to be teachers of the law*, raise against this doctrine, as calculated to feed the pride of self-righteousness; to spread Arminianism; to disparage the grace and merit of Christ; and other things of the same sort. But there is a pride which needs mortification as much as any other, although it escapes their notice; and that is, the pride of conceited ignorance. Little as we incline to flatter vanity, we shall not attack it upon principles which would prostrate along with it the righteousness of God, and cover the pages of his blessed word with contradictions and lies. We hold it to be a maxim almost self-evident, that abounding and impudent wickedness will bring more wrath, and therefore more misery, upon a land, than wickedness shut up in the bosom, or driven, by the commanding aspect of truth, into secret corners. If our citizens, who are perpetually praising Christianity, and perpetually insulting it, were to yield a *decent* deference to its authority—if our magistrates, instead of sacrificing their allegiance to God, whose ministers they are,* on the altar of a wretched and fickle popularity, were to become a more steady and uniform " terrour to evil doers, "the storm which blackens over our trembling country would be dissipated; and the smiling skies invite every man to resume his seat " under his vine and under his fig-tree."

* Rom. xiii.

The preventing of sin, then, being a prevention of misery, the world owes much of its freedom from misery to the influence of the visible church, *constituted as it is*, in restraining sin—more, much more, than it would owe to such a constitution as would exclude all nominal Christians; the number of them who are reconciled to God by the death of his son, remaining the same. We say the number of unconverted remaining the same. For it cannot be doubted, that as two real Christians are better and more useful than one *real* and one *apparent* Christian; so the two latter are much better and more useful than one real Christian, and one openly wicked man. And as, for the same reason, it would be infinitely more desirable, that the whole world should be in the church, and the whole church converted, than that there should be a mixture of clean and unclean in her communion; so it is infinitely more desirable, and more conducive to peace and happiness, that while this purity is unattainable, the appearance of godliness in those who have none, should encourage the hearts and strengthen the hands of those who have it; and thus hypocrisy concur with sincerity in causing " iniquity, as ashamed, to hide her head."

There is another view of this point which comes home to the heart. To that question " Why must believers die ?" The following an-

swer among others, has been returned. If believers were exempted from the common mortali-
ty ; if, like Enoch and Elijah, they should go to
heaven without " putting off their tabernacle,"
then Death would reveal the secrets of the eternal world   It would be known by the very manner of his departing hence, whether an individual
was saved or lost.   What anguish, what horrour,
what distraction, would fill the souls and the families of God's dear children; to be assured, by
the simple fact of a friend or kinsman's dying, that
he was gone to hell! But would not the very
same effect be produced, were all unbelievers
shut out of the church ? The mere circumstance
of their exclusion would prove their unbelief ; and
their death in unbelief, would prove that they had
perished. The tender mercies of God relieve his
people from an intolerable load of suffering, by
subjecting them, in common with others, to the
decree of death. And that constitution of his
visible church, which, by admitting members
upon external evidence, admits hypocrites as well
as the sincere, is a necessary counterpart to the
law of death. Visible departure from the world,
whether into his church or into eternity, lies
through an entrance which God has so construct-
ed, that any farther than a judgment may be
formed from external evidence, he alone " knoweth them that are his." Both are provisions of

one gracious system. They, therefore, who would so model the Christian church as to keep or to expel from her communion, all ungodly men who do not show themselves to be such by their ungodly principles or deeds, are labouring to defeat the mercy displayed in the death of a believer, and to wring his heart with agony during the whole period of his life. Eternal thanks to the divine compassions! They cannot succeed. The counsel of the Lord is against them; and " the counsel of the Lord, *that* shall stand."

3. The mixed character of the church contributes directly to her prosperity. It does so,

By extending her resources:

By increasing her numbers:

By affording protection.

First, The resources of the church, we mean her outward resources, are extended by her present constitution. These, in general, are *pecuniary* aid, and the aid of *talents.*

It is evident, that *all* those means by which the gospel is supported and propagated, are not furnished by real Christians; and equally evident that the whole supply is very scanty. If you should deduct the part which comes from the pockets of unconverted men, the balance would not preserve Christianity from being starved out of the world. Indeed, from the wretched provision which is commonly made for her maintenance, one might conclude, with little offence against charity, that the great majority of professed Christians, are not unwilling to try how far this experiment of *starving* may prove successful. That is their sin, and it shall be their punishment. Let them think of it in those moments when they recollect that they are as accountable for the use of their property, as for the use of their liberty : and that there is to be a day of reckoning, in which no robbers shall appear to less advantage, or be treated with less indulgence, than those, who in this life, have " robbed God."*

But small as the encouragement is for any, who by following another honest calling, can procure a tolerable livelihood, and lay up even a little for their families, to devote themselves to the religious welfare of society, it would be much smaller were none to be accounted Christians here, who shall not be accounted such hereafter. Go, with the power of detecting hypocrisy; cast out of the church, all whose fellowship is not " with the Father, and with his Son, Jesus Christ." And your next step must be to nail up the doors of our places of worship. We are in the habit of praying that the Lord, who has declared that " the silver is his, and the gold is his," would influence the hearts of the opulent to bring their offerings into his courts : We thank him, when,

* Mal. iii. 8, 9.

in a manner somewhat uncommon, he hears our
prayers, and sends the bounty; and yet we overlook the daily occurrence of this very thing which
is the object of our petitions and of our grati-
tude ! He has incorporated the principle in the
frame of his visible church, and it operates with
regular, though silent, efficacy. But if all who
appear to be Christians, and are not, were ex-
cluded, the effect must be to diminish, in a most
distressing degree, the actual pecuniary resources
of the church. For men who are marked as enemies, will never lend her the same aid as men
who are supposed to be friends. And thus the
absolute purification of the church upon earth,
would overthrow the plan which the wisdom of
God has devised, to cause his very foes to assess
their own purses in carrying on that dispensation
of grace which, at heart, they do not love; and
which, if left to themselves, they would resist
with all their might.

The same reason applies to *talent.*

Revelation is never more completely robed in
light, than when she is brought fairly and fully to
the bar of evidence. The attacks of infidels
have furnished her friends with both opportunities
and incitements to dispel the mist by which she
has been occasionally or partially obscured ; and
she has gone forth " fair as the moon, clear as the
sun, and terrible as an army with banners."

What is true of Christianity in general, is equal
ly true of its peculiar doctrines. The more rigid-
ly they are examined, the more worthy do they
appear of God; the more perfectly adapted to the
condition of man; the more consistent with each
other, with the lights of pure philosophy, and the
discoveries of real science.

But these results which have shed, and are
shedding, their lustre upon the evangelical system, combine the researches of the ablest men
in the most·literary periods of the world. There
is no department of human knowledge which God
has not laid under tribute to his word. Linguists,
mathematicians, astronomers, botanists, mineral-
ogists; chymistry, physiology, and medicine; the
antiquarian, the traveller, the natural, civil, and
ecclesiastical historian; commerce, agriculture,
mechanics, and the fine arts—are all to be found
waiting at the temple of God, opening their treasures, and presenting their gifts. Whoever has
the least acquaintance with things older than
himself, and without the petty circle of his personal agency, knows that the mass of all valuable
learning, since the introduction of Christianity,
ever has been, and is yet, in the hands of professed
Christians. They have employed it in her de-
fence, to an extent and with an effect of which
thousands, who are now reaping the benefits of
their efforts, can have no possible conception.

Yet, certainly, among those who have thus fortified the citadel of truth, many were believers in
name only, and never tasted the salvation to the
influence of which they contributed. " How much
better," you will exclaim, " had they loved the
Redeemer not in name only, but in deed and in
truth !" How much better indeed ! But how
much worse, we rejoin, had they sided with his
open enemies, and levelled *against* his word, all
that artillery which they employed *for* it. And
that such would have been the consequence
had none been admitted into his church, who
were not partakers of his grace, is as evident,
as that a cause, left to its own operation, will
produce its proper effect. We are well apprised of the contempt which some men affect
to heap upon human learning. And we are
equally well apprised that in this their hostility
their ignorance and vain glory have at least as
large a share as their spirituality of mind. Nor
are we regardless of the mischief which " unsanctified learning" has done in the church of God;
and of the jealousy with which, on that account,
many serious people look upon learned men. But
why ? Shall we never distinguish between *use* and
abuse ? Learning is good in itself. The evil lies
not in its nature, but in its application. Because
some have prostituted their learning to pervert the truth and institutions of our Lord Jesus

Christ, shall we not accept the aid of the same weapon, rightfully used, to vindicate them ? Shall we commit them to the illiterate and the stupid, in expectation of miracles to elicit wisdom from the mouth of folly ? and bribe letters and genius to enlist themselves in the service of the devil ? The very same objection strikes at wealth, at strength; at every power, moral and physical, which God has seen fit to create. Because " unsanctified" opulence has spread corruption through Christian communities, is it desirable that all Christians be beggars ? Because strong men, if they be of quarrelsome temper, may keep a whole neighbourhood under the terrours of assault and battery, would it therefore be desirable that all Christians should be pigmies ? It is the nature of every thing to work harm when misdirected, in exact proportion to its power of working good when directed well. This is a law of God's own enacting : and is one of the means by which he makes sin to punish itself. Therefore, to reject a potent agency because its perversion will involve calamity proportioned to its vigour, is the very rectified spirit of absurdity. Carry your principle through; and tell your maker that he did a foolish thing in creating angels, because such of them as, by their fall, have become devils, can do infinitely more mischief than if they had been men ! No—Let us put away these childish things. If unconverted men get into the church under the cloak of a credible profession; if they remain there undetected; if they bring their wealth and their talent to the support of the Christian cause, let us accept the boon with all thankfulness. It is so much of the arm of iniquity palsied; nay, more, it is so much clear gain from the interests of hell to the comforter of the church of God. If the gospel is to be maintained, or a starving disciple to be fed, it will make no difference in the market whether the dollar was given by a hypocrite or a believer. And if the bible be happily illustrated; or its adversaries victoriously encountered, the truth is still the same, whether the talent which demonstrates it be connected with the spirit of faith or the heart of unbelief. The excess of these two benefits over and above what could be performed by Christians alone, is the advantage, in point of *resource*, which the church derives from her present constitution, over and above that which she would enjoy were none to enter into her communion but true converts.

The *second* way in which the mixed character of the visible church contributes directly to her prosperity, is by *increasing her numbers.*

The gospel is the great means of turning men *from darkness to light, and from the power of Satan unto God.* For this purpose it is necessary that they and it should meet. *How shall they call on* *him in whom they have not believed? And how shall they believe in him of whom they have not heard? And how shall they hear without a preacher?*[*] What-ever brings sinners within the reach of the means of salvation, and places them under the " joyful sound," puts them into the way in which alone they have a right to expect the pardoning and the renewing mercy of their God. Let it, then, be considered, how many members of the external church have remained for years in their habit of decent but unprofitable attendance upon the pub-lic worship of God, and have at last been arrest-ed by his grace, and *made heirs according to the hope of eternal life.* " Their number," it may be objected, " is smaller than we suppose; and forms too inconsiderable a portion of the saved to have any weight in the argument."

We believe this, upon the whole, to be true. It was long ago observed, and the observation ought to sink down into the hearts of both the old and young professor, that where the gospel is enjoyed in its purity, it is the ordinary method of provi-dence to call sinners into the fellowship of Jesus Christ in the *days of their youth.* Among those who have enjoyed from their childhood the benefit of religious instruction, of holy example, of sound and faithful ministrations, the instances of conver-sion after middle life, are, for the most part, ex-

* Rom. x. 14.

tremely rare.   Let the aged Christian run over,
in his mind, such of these instances as have come
within his own knowledge, and we shall be much
deceived if his list be not very short.   Yet small
as is their *relative* number, their amount, absolutely taken, is not contemptible.   But had a
power of judging the state of the soul before God,
from other than external evidence, been the rule
of admission into his church, who can doubt that
the rejection of these members would have
banished the most of them from his sanctuary altogether, and left them to perish in their iniquity.
It is vain to reply that " *the Lord knoweth them that
are his,* and will take care that none of them be
lost."   He *does* know them : he *will* take care that
none of them be lost ; but he will reveal his
knowledge and exercise his care, by the intervention of means : and the admission of members
into his church upon external evidence *only*, appears, from the nature of the thing, and is proved
by the event, to be one of his means.

The operation, however, of this cause of her increase, is not confined to the persons of late converts : nor would our argument be much affected,
were they still fewer, or were there none at all.
Thousands, who *have the form of godliness without
the power,* and who die as they live, *in the gall of
bitterness and the bond of iniquity,* are heads of families.   By their authority and example, children,

apprentices, servants, who, otherwise, would rove
unrestrained like *the wild asses colt*, are kept from
much gross and open wickedness : they learn to
respect the sabbath day; they come under Christian instruction ; they attend the institutions of
public worship; to multitudes of them God blesses
his own ordinances for their eternal life.   And
thus, while the parent or the master dies in his
sin, the child, the apprentice, or the servant, led
by his own hand to the religious precept and the
house of prayer, becomes an *heir of God, and a fellow heir with Christ in glory.*   Nay, individuals
without families, are often the unconscious instruments of salvation to others.   No human being is
so poor as not to have an acquaintance.   We
know it to be a principle in human nature, that
men love to draw their friends into connexions
with which they themselves are pleased.   It is a
necessary effect of man's social character; and is
no where more regular and extensive than in his
religious associations.   Many causes beside, and
without, conversion from sin to God, render men
zealous in promoting the credit and prosperity of
their respective churches.   The prejudice of birth,
the force of habit, the preference of judgment, attachment to a particular minister or circle of
friends, engage much warm and active patronage
to ecclesiastical bodies.   One companion brings
another; that one a third; and thus, by a most

complicated system of individual action and re-
action, great multitudes are assembled in the
house of God, who otherwise would never cross
its threshold. Sometimes a person, induced by
the persuasion of another to hear a certain
preacher, or occupy a seat in a certain church,
has been awakened to a sense of eternal things ;
has been " translated into the kingdom of God's
dear Son ;" and sealed up by the holy spirit of
promise, unto the day of redemption," when his
persuader has remained unmoved, or even thrown
away his profession, and turned an open reprobate.

Withdraw, then, all the families of nominal
Christians, and all their acquaintances whom they
allure to the public ordinances—withdraw the acquaintances of single men and women, especially
those in younger life, and after you have made
the deduction, look at your places of worship !
Whole rows of seats which were filled with
persons of decent, respectful, and even serious
deportment, are empty. The greater part of those
from whom converts were to be drawn to replace
dying believers, and perpetuate the knowledge of
Jesus and the resurrection, is gone. The church
has lost one of her chief holds upon the world :
she has closed up a wide door of her own access
to unbelievers ; and has actually banished them,
by hundreds, from the mercy-seat.

There is an exception to this reasoning too obvious and plausible to pass unnoticed.

" Facts appear to be against us. Who composed the audiences of the apostles ? Who flocked to the sound of the evangelical trumpet, at the blessed reformation from popery ? What is, at this day, the most successful method of crowding the churches, even with those who do not so much as profess to be religious? Is it not the plain and undisguised declaration of that very gospel which, it is said, the people will not hear without the help of hypocrites to bring them. If you want to empty a place of worship, court your Christians in name only; let nothing be done to shock their prejudices or alarm their pride. If you want to fill a place of worship, *know nothing* in your ministrations *but Jesus Christ, and him crucified.*"

A mistake is never so imposing as when it misapplies undoubted truths. We admit all the facts here stated, but cannot see how they invalidate our reasoning. Because they have occurred in the history of the church, so conducted as not to exclude the secret deceiver. Her character has always been mixed. The pretensions of some men to purify her in such a manner as to admit only genuine converts, are vanity and wind. They never did, they never can, it is impossible, in the nature of things, they ever should, act upon other than external evidence, if they act upon evidence

at all.   Could a method be devised of distinguishing the *real* from the *apparent* Christian, not only
would it cease to be the Lord's prerogative " to
know them that are his;" but the whole com-
plexion and character of his church would be altered. ' She would be *another church altogether from
what he has made her.*   And since he has adapted
the tenour of his providence, and the influences of
his grace, to her *actual constitution*, it is idle to
imagine that the course of events which is connected with her *present* constitution, would attend
her under a constitution *essentially different.*   The
church, framed as some good men would have
her, not only never existed, but, for aught they
can show, would be utterly unfit for this world of
ours ; and would utterly fail of accomplishing her
ends.   Nor can they assign any tolerable reason
for a belief that of all the effects which *now* flow
from the dispensation of the gospel, a *single one*
would be produced upon a change of the system.

An advantage, therefore, and not a small one,
of the mixed condition of the church is, that it
collects within her pale, and introduces to her ordinances, multitudes who otherwise would remain
" without," but, now, "shall be heirs of salvation."

A *third* benefit directly arising from the mixed
condition of the church, is *protection.*

In times of affliction, the witnesses for truth are
often more, and in the times of prosperity fewer,

than they are supposed to be. Could the line be accurately drawn between sound and unsound professors, the former would frequently find themselves in a very small minority. Such a disclosure would not only dispirit their minds and repress their exertions, but subject them to taunt, to insult, and to oppression. We must bear in remembrance that the " world which lieth in wickedness," never wants the inclination to persecute them who are " chosen out of it." The *computed* number of Christians serves to check that inclination; and it is often checked so effectually that its existence is denied; and Christians themselves are half persuaded, that the world is less hostile to them and their master than in the days of primitive peril. But could they be distinctively pointed out, this erring charity of theirs would get its rebuke in their ruin. The fire would feed upon their flesh, and scaffolds stream with their blood, at the instance, and by the agency, of many who now treat them with civility and respect. Set them up as a mark, by exposing their weakness, and nothing short of a perpetual miracle would hinder " the men of the earth" from exterminating them at a stroke, and, with them, the church of the living God.

But as the case stands, his overruling providence uses the nominal, for a shield to the real, Christian. Apparent believers occupy a middle

ground between the church of the redeemed and
the world which knows not God. Belonging in
pretence to the one, and in fact to the other, they
interpose a medium between the two, which often
prevents a destructive contact.

The malice of the persecutor sleeps, and his
arm is idle, from the difficulty of selecting his victim and pointing his blow. Were he to strike at
random, he would smite those whom he wishes
to spare, and miss those whom he wishes to smite.
Thus there is a secret, and silent, but real and ef-
fective, alliance between unconverted men in the
church and out of it, which the controlling hand
of God makes to subserve the safety and comfort
of his own people.

Such are some of the ends, "holy, just, and
good," which we, circumscribed as is our knowledge of the ways of God, can perceive to be accomplished by the mixed condition of his church.
That there are no others most worthy of his wisdom, though infinitely above the reach of ours, nothing but inebriating folly will dare to pronounce.
What ultimate relations his church may have to
his universal kingdom, it were impertinent, if
not profane, so much as to conjecture. Suffice it
that while every step of our progress enjoins so-
briety of thought; restrains the indiscretion of
zeal; and rebukes the spirit of intrusive igno-

rance; enough is discovered to remove the modest scruple, and satisfy the reverential inquiry.

In a preceding part of this discussion, we contracted an engagement which we shall here fulfil.

To our doctrine which unequivocally admits that the visible church is so constituted as to contain a mixture of good men and bad, without any means of distinguishing, precisely, the one from the other; and which maintains that the infants of parents, or a parent, professing godliness, are, by the fact of their birth, members of the church, and intitled to the sacramental seal of their relation, it is objected, that " we debase and prostitute the sacraments; that we necessarily give the seal of spiritual blessings to multitudes who have not and never shall have, " any inheritance in the kingdom of Christ and of God"—that by such an application we not only put a seal to a blank, which is mere mockery; but call upon the God of Truth to certify a lie, which is yet worse than mockery— that it is peculiarly absurd to administer to infants an ordinance coupled by the scriptures with faith in Christ, which infants are confessedly incapable of exercising."

This is specious, and well calculated to gain the popular ear. In reasoning, as in other things, it is commonly much easier to get into a difficulty than to get out of it. Objections to any fixed order are always at hand, because its operation is always felt: but answers to those objections are not so ready, because the reasons of the order cease to be observed, as time is always removing them further from our knowledge. On this account it frequently requires more sense and search to refute one cavil, than to propose twenty. From the same cause minds which feel the force of the cavil, are, in thousands of instances, unable to comprehend the refutation, even though it be mathematically correct. Hence shrewd, but petty sophism, and warm but cloudy declamation, against the visible church, make a quick impression, and exert a lasting influence, upon the weak, the illiterate, and the vain; while the reply to them can hardly hope to succeed, except among those who are capable of thinking; and among whom their progress is small, their proselytes few, and their dominion tottering.

In the present case there appears to have been, and to be, a peculiar infatuation. It has been demonstrated over and over, that the common, which are the strongest, objections to the doctrine of a visible church catholic, in so far at least, as it embraces the administration of the sacraments, apply with equal force to the system of their advocates ; to an appointment unquestionably divine ; and to the scriptural declarations concerning eternal life.

1. To the system of their advocates.

For if the baptising of infants who possibly may not, and, in many instances, certainly do not, prove to be true Christians, is chargeable with nullity and mockery; then the baptising of adults who possibly may not, and, in many instances, certainly do not, prove to be true Christians, is equally a nullity and a mockery: And therefore, unless we can know who shall be the heirs of salvation, and restrict the sacraments accordingly, their administration must always be involved in the charge of nullity and mockery. The opponents of infant baptism are so pinched by this retortion of their argument, that they endeavour to disembarrass themselves by adopting the *reality* of Christian experience, that is, the *discovery* of a man's gracious state, as their principle of admission to sacramental privilege. The subterfuge will not avail them. They must found their discovery either on special revelation, or upon other evidence. To the former they cannot pretend; and the latter they must derive from one of two sources: either the fruits of grace in a man's life, which must be certified by others, and are *external evidence ;* or the account which he himself gives of his own conversion. This to himself is *internal,* but the moment he mentions it to others, it becomes *testimony,* and like the former, it is *external* evidence.

Is, then, the judgment of his examiners liable to mistake? If not, how did they become infallible?

And, as the reality of a gracious state is the reason of their admitting a man into their communion, it must for ever remain a sufficient reason for retaining him: for those with whom we now contend, hold the doctrine of the perseverance of the saints.   How, then, can they ever justify the exclusion of any of their members? For as the possession of grace is the ground of his admission, nothing but the want of it can be a ground of his expulsion.   Thus, in every case of excommunication, they stand self-convicted of having mistaken a man's character either when they took him in, or when they cast him out. From this alternative they have no escape but an acknowledgment that they were either faithless in the first instance, or tyrannical in the second.   In so far, therefore, as they have ever had their communion, members, who, when " weighed in the balances, were found wanting," it is impossible not to perceive that they are in very same predicament with those whom they reproach as lax and carnal, that in the same proportion their own sacraments are nullities and mockeries; and that their blow at the advocates of the one visible church, recoils, with all its force, upon their own heads.

2. Their objections to our doctrine, are equally conclusive against an appointment unquestionably divine: we mean the ordinance of *circumcision.*

We must repeat, that as circumcision is expressly declared to be a " seal of the righteousness of faith;" and as it was applied by God's own commandment to infants eight days old, if the baptism of infants who know nothing of believing in Christ, is nullity and mockery ; an absurd and foolish ceremony : *then*, the circumcision of infants who knew nothing of that righteousness of faith which it sealed, was also a nullity and a mockery ; was also an absurd and foolish ceremony ; and the divine commandment which enjoined it, a foolish and an absurd commandment.

3. These same objections are applicable to the scriptural doctrine of eternal life. " *He that* BE-LIEVETH and is BAPTIZED, shall be *saved*," quotes the Anabaptist. We continue the quotation : " *But he that* BELIEVETH NOT, *shall be* DAMNED.*

His argument is this :
Faith is required in order to baptism :
But infants cannot exercise faith :
Therefore, infants cannot be baptised.
We turn his argument thus :
Faith is required in order to salvation :
But infants cannot exercise faith :
Therefore, infants cannot be saved.

And so this famous syllogism begins with shut-

* Mark xvi. 16.

ting out our children from the church of God;
and ends with consigning all of them who die in
infancy to the damnation of hell!*

We are quite weary and almost ashamed of
repeating answers so trite as those which we are
compelled to repeat, against still more trite objections; but it is of importance to show that the
heaviest stroke which the enemies of our doctrine level at us, is leveled, with equal strength,
at themselves, their bible, and their God.

These remarks belong to that sort of argument
which is called *argumentum ad hominem:* that is,
an argument drawn from a man's own principles
against himself. Its use is, not so much to prove
the truth, as to disprove errour: not to show that
our own cause is good; but that our adversary's
reasoning is bad; by showing that his weapon cannot pierce us but at the expense of transfixing
himself: so that if he prevail against us, he will,

---

* We do not say that the opposers of infant baptism hold such
an opinion. Their most distinguished writers disown and repel
it. But we say, that it necessarily results from their requiring
faith, in *all* cases, as a qualification for baptism. They do not
follow out their own position. They stop short at the point which
suits their system. We take it up where they leave it, and conduct it to its direct and inevitable conclusion. Therefore, though
we do not charge the *men* with maintaining that those who die in
infancy, perish; yet we charge this consequence upon their *argument :* For it certainly proves this, or it proves nothing at all.

in the moment of his victory, meet his own death
on the point of his own sword.

We owe our readers more. We owe a decision on the merits of the case. Which we shall
attempt by pointing out the true use of the sacramental seal.

We observed, in an early part of the discussion,
that the difficulty which produces objections like
those we have been exposing, is created by erroneous notions of the church of God; by confounding visible members with his elect; and his covenant to the church with his covenant of grace in
Christ Jesus; and that a proper application of
this distinction will remove the difficulty.*

The sacramental seal has appropriate relations
to these covenants respectively, and thus we distinguish them.

1. It has visible relations to the visible church.
Particularly,

(1.) It certifies, that the covenant of her God
to her abides, and secures to her the perpetual
enjoyment of her covenanted privileges.

(2.) It certifies, that the righteousness of faith
and the salvation connected with it, are dispensed
in the church; and that there, and there alone,
they are to be expected and sought.

(3.) It certifies, that the church is under the
consecration of the redeemer's blood; has an un-

No. IV. p. 83.

ceasing interest in his mediation; and access in her public character, and in the acts of direct worship, to "the holiest of all."

(4.) It certifies, that the covenanted seed shall never be extinct; but that "a seed shall serve the Lord Jesus, and shall be accounted to him for a generation, so long as the sun and the moon endure."

(5.) It certifies that in the ordinary course of his providence, God will cause his saving mercy to run in the channel of his people's families.

(6.) It certifies, that the individual sealed is himself a link in the great chain for transmitting down, from generation to generation, the knowledge and execution of God's plan of grace.

(7.) It certifies, that the individual sealed has a right to the prayers, the instruction, the protection, and the discipline of the house of God.

(8.) In the baptism of infants, it certifies, that even *they* need the purification of that blood " which cleanses from all sin ;" and that it *can be applied* to them for their salvation. So that infant baptism is a visible testimony, incorporated with the ordinances of God's worship, both to the guilt and depravity of our nature independently on actual transgression, and to the only remedy through our Lord Jesus Christ. If you reject it, you throw away the *only ordinance* which *directly* asserts the principle upon which the whole fabric of redemption is built, viz. that we are *by nature children of wrath.*

These are great and important uses of the sacramental seal; intimately connected with the faith, hope, and consolation of the church; and yet distinct and separate from an individual's interest in the salvation of God. Whatever shall become of him, they are grand, and solemn, and tender truths to which he is the instrument of perpetuating a testimony. Should he afterwards be a reproach, instead of an ornament, to the gospel; should he be " abominable, and disobedient, and to every good work reprobate," he shall perish indeed ;· but his perdition shall not affect the testimony given in his person, by the sacramental seal, to those blessed truths and privileges which we have enumerated. That testimony, that *sealed* testimony, is absolute; it is perfectly independent upon his spiritual state ; and is precisely the same, whether he be " appointed to wrath, or to obtain salvation by our Lord Jesus Christ."

2. The sacramental seal has a special relation to the church invisible, and to the spiritual mercies of the covenant of grace.

Union with Christ; acceptance in his merits ; participation of his Spirit ; the fellowship of his death, of the power of his resurrection, of his everlasting love, and an interest in all the blessings of his purchase, the sacraments do certainly represent and seal. These glorious objects always have been, and still are, in the most lively and affecting manner, exhibited to, and perceived by, the faith of believers; and their personal interest therein is at times certified to their consciences by " that holy spirit of promise whereby they are sealed to the day of redemption." But all this is peculiar to the household of faith. It presupposes their interest in Christ; it is over and above the *general* uses which we just now specified; and is a secret between the omniscient God and the happy recipient.

The reader now sees, that the attestation of the sacramental seal is to be limited and extended by the *state of the receiver.* If he be only a member of the visible church, and merely within the bond of the external covenant, it certifies *in* him and *to* him whatever appertains to him in that relation, and nothing more. But if he be a member of the church invisible also, and interested in the saving benefits of the covenant of grace; it goes further, and certifies whatever appertains to him in *that* relation.

With the help of this obvious distinction we remove difficulties which are otherwise extremely perplexing; reconcile expressions otherwise irreconcileable; show the futility of objections founded on the want of grace in the individual sealed;

and demonstrate, as we promised, " *that the seal of God's covenant does, in every instance, certify absolute truth ; whether it be applied to a believer or an unbeliever ; to the elect or the reprobate.*"

CHURCH OF GOD.

No. VII.

Results.

FROM explaining the *uses* which the visible church, constituted as we have stated it to be, subserves, we pass on to some of its practical *results*. We mean certain principles, flowing, as necessary conclusions, from the doctrine which we have established; and which directly influence the whole system of ecclesiastical order.

1. The right and duty of *all them who in every place call upon the name of the Lord Jesus*, to hold religious fellowship with each other, as God affordeth opportunity, are undisputed among Christians. Whatever be their diversities of opinion concerning the extent of that general description, and the religious fellowship founded upon it, yet within the limits which they prescribe to themselves respectively, they not only revere it as a duty, but esteem it as a privilege: They both insist upon its letter, and act in its spirit. A private

Christian goes from one congregation to another, and is received upon the evidence of his having been a member of that which he left. A minister of the gospel travels into parts distant from the place and society where he was ordained; and preaches the word, without scruple, in any other part of the world; and without a thought of his wanting a new commission. A person lawfully baptized is every where considered as under sacramental consecration to God in Christ; and nobody dreams of repeating his baptism. We make no account of the question about a valid or invalid ministry, because we confine ourselves, at present, to the communion which obtains among those who are agreed on this point.

We ask, then, what is the origin and reason of this communion? What is there to render it lawful and proper? "A common interest," you will say, "in the Christian ordinances, and the benefits dispensed by them." No doubt. But what is the basis of this common interest? How did it become common? "Christ has procured it for his church." Most certainly. But *what* church? The church of those who are "written in the Lamb's book of life?" Nothing more incontrovertible. Yet do you not perceive that you have laid the foundation of all religious fellowship in this—that the elect church of the redeemed is ONE? and that individual Christians enjoy their spiritual immunities, merely as *parts of that great whole* to which Christ has bequeathed them ? As members of the *one* " household of faith ?" As citizens of the *one* " city of God ?" That the right to spiritual privileges turns precisely on this point, " They are given to the church, and I am a member of the church." But as there can be no external communion without an external church, and as all the sections of true believers all the world over, compose but one church invisible, it follows that the sections, or if you will, congregations, of visible believers, compose but one visible church. For it seems unreasonable to say, that the *whole* number of real Christians should not bear the same general relation to the *whole* number of professing Christians among whom they are included, with that which every *portion* of real Christians bears to that *portion* of professed Christians in which it is included. But the relation which a number of true Christians, in the bonds of Christian fellowship, bear to the external society to which they belong, is that of a *part* of the Church catholic invisible, to a *particular* visible church. Therefore, the relation which all the parts of the church invisible bear to all particular visible churches, is that of one general church invisible to one general church visible.

Again: The several portions of real Christians are related to their aggregate number, as *parts of*

a great whole which is the Catholic church invisible.   Therefore, all the portions or congregations
of professed Christians are related to each other
as *parts of a great whole*, which is the Catholic
church visible.

Hence it results, that as a right to those privileges which the Lord Jesus hath purchased for his
redeemed, is founded in the circumstance of being
a member of that church which is made up of
them; so, a right to the external privileges which
are dispensed by an external ministry in the external church is founded upon the fact of one's
being a member of that church.   It is on this
ground, and on this alone, that the communion of
churches is established.   A man is not admitted
to Christian fellowship in one congregation because he is a member of another—this would be
a solecism.   But he is admitted because he is a
member of *the* church catholic; of which his communion in *any* particular church is received as
evidence by every *other* particular church.   He is
free of the " city of God," and therefore entitled
to the immunities of citizenship in whatever part
of the city he may happen to be.   We may illustrate this matter by an analogy from civil affairs.
A citizen of the state of New-York carries his
citizenship with him to every spot under her jurisdiction.   It is of no consequence in what county
or town he resides ; nor how often he removes

from one town or county to another; nor whether he be at his own dwelling; or on a visit to a friend; or on a journey; whatever privileges belong to him in his general character of a citizen of the state, he can claim any where and every where: for example, the right of voting for governour, provided he be legally qualified.

On the contrary, a man's being an inhabitant of a particular city or town, does not give him the least title to the immunities peculiar to any other city or town. It would be very absurd for him to insist that because he had a right to vote for charter-officers in New-York, therefore he has a right to vote for charter-officers in Albany! The reason is, they are independent on each other. But if voting for charter-officers were a right attached to citizenship at large, then he could claim the right in any city within the state—and he would vote in Albany, not because he had voted in New-York, but because he is a member of the *state* which includes them both.

The very same principle pervades the church of God. Were it not *one*, no man could claim privilege or exercise office, out of the particular church to which he belongs. A minister is no minister out of his own pulpit and his own charge. It would be just as proper for an alderman of New-York to issue writs in Albany, as for a minister of a congregation in New-York to offer to preach in Albany. The effect would be, that a minister must have a new commission, that is, a new ordination, for every new church he should preach in.

We know that no church under heaven is able to carry this principle out into practice. There is but one of two ways to avoid the embarrassment:

Either, communion between the members and ministers of different congregations, is the result of an agreement between them; or the independent churches themselves do act upon the principle which they deny, the catholic unity of the church.

If the latter, our point is gained. If the former, then the communion of churches is derived, not from their communion with our Lord Jesus Christ, nor from his authority; but from a *human compact;* and thus far we have no *Christian* privileges at all.

If, to elude the force of this conclusion, it be said, that Christ has warranted and required his churches, although independent of each other, to keep up their fellowship in his name—we reply, that this is a contradiction. Because the very fact of his uniting them in such fellowship constitutes them, to its whole extent, but *one body*, the members of which cannot possibly be independent on each other. The issue is, that all Christian and ministerial communion originates in the visible unity of the catholic church; and that tnere is no explaining its reason, nor preserving its existence, without admitting, in some shape or other, that the church of God is *one*—this is our *first* result.

2. From the relation in which the children of believing parents stand in the church of God there result mutual rights and duties.

1st. Such children have a *right*, even in their infancy, to a solemn acknowledgment of their membership by the administration of baptism— they have a right to the individual and collective prayers of Christians; that is to be remembered before the throne of grace by Christians in their retired devotion, and in the public worship of the church.—They have a right, during their tender age, to her instruction, her protection, and her salutary control. It would be strange, indeed, if little children, who were so graciously noticed by her king and her God, should have no claim upon her parental affection. They are her hope; they are the seed from which she is to look for " trees of righteousness; the planting of JEHOVAH that he may be glorified." And, as such, they are intitled to her patient and assiduous culture.

This is the birth-right of the children of those who name the name of the Lord Jesus. We had it from our fathers. " They trusted in God; they trusted in him and they were not confounded." He was their God; and he was our God also, be-

cause he was the God of their seed.   Thus " the
lines fell unto us in pleasant places ; yea we had
a goodly heritage."   Owning the God of our fathers, we call upon him as the God of our seed;
and the inheritance which we derived from them
we transmit to our sons and our daughters, that
they may hand it down to their children, and their
children to another generation.   Our giddy youth
undervalue this privilege; our profane youth laugh
at it.   In doing so they " observe lying vanities,
and forsake their own mercies."   Such as have
come to their right mind, and have learned to sit
at the feet of Jesus, will say, with heartfelt emotion, in the words of Dr. Watts :

> " Lord, I ascribe it to thy grace ;
>   And not to chance, as others do ;
> That I was born of Christian race,
>   And not a heathen or a Jew."

2d. There are *duties* corresponding with these
privileges.   Youth born in the Christian church,
acknowledged as her children, and put under her
care, can never shake off certain tender and solemn obligations.

They are bound to revere her authority, and to
promote her happiness.   The very law of nature
intitles her to this.   A young man who should
evince, from the time he was capable of action, a
studied contempt for the magistrates, laws, institutions and welfare of his country, would be held

to have renounced all virtuous principle; and, if he should elude the tribunals of justice, could not escape the punishment of public detestation. But why? Is it because God has entrusted his church with his living oracles; and dignified her with his gracious presence, that her counsels are beneath regard, and her control a matter of scorn? Is it because she has done more to prepare her children for usefulness, for comfort, and for glory, than mere civil society ever did, or ever can do, that she has forfeited their esteem, does not deserve a hearing when she exhorts or remonstrates, and shall have her most friendly and faithful services repaid with indifference or disdain? And shall behaviour which, in every other community would seal a man up for infamy, be applauded as spirited and magnanimous in the church of God? Let not the unworthy notion find a place among our young people; let them feel their obligation to requite, with kindness, the care which watched over their early days; and to respect the counsels and institutions whose tendency is not to debase, but to ennoble them; not to embitter their enjoyments, but to ensure their peace; not to lead them into harm, but to save them from ruin here, and to crown them with external blessedness in the world to come.

Let them reflect, moreover, that they are bound to own their relation to the church of God, by professing the name of the Lord Jesus Christ; showing forth his death in the communion of the holy supper, and walking in all his ordinances and commandments blameless.

It is to be feared that even such of them as are of sober deportment; as carefully avoid every thing rude or unbecoming toward Christianity and Christians ; as would turn with horrour from open infidelity, do yet, for the most part, labour under the evil of an erroneous conscience on this subject; and seduce themselves into a false and hurtful tranquillity. They seem to think that professing or not professing to be followers of Christ is a matter of mere choice—that the omission contracts no guilt, while it enlarges the sphere of their indulgences, and exempts them from the necessity of that tender and circumspect walk which belongs to a real Christian.

This is all wrong—radically wrong. The very mildest construction which it can bear, amounts to a confession of their being " aliens from the commonwealth of Israel and strangers to the covenants of promise"—of their anxiety to decline something which the service of God imposes, or of retaining something which it abjures—and is not *this* a most alarming thought ? Do they expect to get to heaven with tempers and habits which are incompatible with devotedness to God upon earth ? If they do not choose to " name the name

of Christ," is it not because they do not choose to
" depart from iniquity?" Let them not cherish
any delusive hope. *Without holiness no man shall
see the Lord. And if any man have not the Spirit of
Christ, he is none of his!* O let them weigh well the
alternative! If they do, what possible reason can
they assign for refusing to honour him before
men? Nay, this cannot be admitted: for if *with
the heart they believe unto righteousness, with the mouth
they will* also *make confession unto salvation.* And
Christ has told them that if they will *not confess
him before men*, they have nothing to expect but
that *he will not confess them before his Father who is
in heaven.* By not confessing the Lord Jesus,
they declare themselves willing to be accounted
unbelievers. Are they prepared for the consequences?

Furthermore. It arises out of the very nature
of the case, that if the most High God condescends
to offer eternal life, in his dear Son, to sinners
whom he might justly shut up under an irreversi-
ble sentence of death, they cannot slight his offer
without the most flagrant ingratitude, and the
most aggravated guilt. His *commandment* to receive the Lord Jesus Christ, as his " unspeakable
gift," is peremptory: and disobedience to it an act
of direct rebellion. To say then, " I will not profess the name of Christ," is to say, " I will neither
submit to the authority of God, nor accept the gift

of his grace." With the very same propriety
might you say, I will pay no respect to the moral
law—I will go after strange Gods: I will bow to
graven images—I will swear and blaspheme—I
will not keep holy the Sabbath day—I will not
obey my parents—I will murder, and commit
adultery, and steal, and lie, and covet; I will do
nothing which God has required; and I will do
every thing which he has forbidden! Does the
youthful reader start and tremble ? Why ? The
same God who has said, Thou shalt not kill—thou
shalt not commit adultery—thou shalt not steal—
thou shalt not lie; has said, *Believe on the Lord Je-*
sus Christ. It is the same authority which enjoins,
and the same rebellion which resists. Thou canst
not, therefore, decline that " good confession, but
at the peril of putting away from thee the words
of eternal life." And thou knowest what his word
has decided.—*If any man love not the Lord Jesus*
Christ, let him be ————.*

There is something more. Many young persons
imagine that they are not members of the church,
until, upon a personal profession of their faith, they
join it in the communion of the holy supper. This
is a great mistake. The children of Christian
parents are *born* members of the church. Their
baptism is founded upon their membership; and
not, as some people suppose, their membership

* 1 Cor. xvi. 22.

upon their baptism. On the same principle, when they arrive at the years of discretion, they may, in taking upon them their baptismal engagements, by a becoming profession of the Lord Jesus, *demand* a seat at his table, as their *privilege* which the church cannot deny. Their allegiance to him as their Redeemer, their King, and their God, is inseparable from their birth-right. The question, then, with them, when they reach that period of maturity which qualifies them to judge for themselves, is, *not* whether they shall contract or avoid an allegiance which has hitherto had no claims upon them : but whether they shall acknowledge or *renounce* an allegiance under which they drew their first breath ? Whether they shall disown the prince of life, and wave their interest in his church ? Whether they shall disclaim the God of their fathers; forswear their consecration to his service— take back the vows which were made over them and for them when they were presented to him in his sanctuary; his blessed name called upon them; and the symbol of that " blood which cleanseth from all sin," applied to them ? Not whether they shall be simple *unbelievers*, but whether they shall display their unbelief in the form of *apostasy ? That* is the question: and an awful one it is. As they value their eternal life, let them consider, that every hour of their continuance in their neglect of Christ is an hour of contempt for his salvation, and of slander on his cross. How shall their hearts endure or their hands be made strong, when he shall come to reckon with them for their *treading him under foot, and counting the blood of the covenant wherewith he was sanctified, an unholy thing?* Reckon with them he will, and precisely for their *not owning him ;* for they cannot, no, they cannot shake off their obligations to own him; although in the attempt they may destroy themselves for ever.

" According to this representation," I shall be told, " the condition of many of our youth is very deplorable. It is their *duty*, you say, to profess the name of Christ, and to seal their profession at the sacramental table. This they cannot do: for they are conscious that they do not possess those principles and dispositions which are requisite to render such a profession honest. What course shall they steer ? If they do not profess Christ, they live in rebellion against God : if they do, they mock him with a lie. Which side of the alternative shall they embrace ? Continue among the profane, and be consistently wicked ? or withdraw from them in appearance, and play the hypocrite ?"

The case is, indeed, very deplorable. Destruction is on either hand. For the UNBELIEVING *shall have their part in the lake of fire,** and *the* HYPO-

* Rev. xxi. 8.

CRITE's *hope shall perish.** God forbid that we should encourage either a false profession, or a refusal to make one. The duty is to embrace *neither* side of the alternative. Not to continue with the profane, and not to act the hypocrite; but to receive the Lord Jesus Christ in truth, and to walk in him. "I cannot do it," replies one: and one, it may be, not without moments of serious and tender emotion upon this very point: "I *cannot* do it." My soul bleeds for thee, thou unhappy! But it *must* be done, or thou art lost for ever. Yet what is the amount of that expression: in the mouth of some a flaunting excuse, and of others a bitter complaint—I cannot? Is the inability to believe in Christ different from an inability to perform any other duty? Is there any harder necessity of calling the God of Truth *a* LIAR, in *not believing the record which he hath given of his* SON, than of committing any other sin? The inability created, the necessity imposed, by the ENMITY *of the carnal mind against God?†* It is the inability of wickedness, and nothing else. Instead of being an apology, it is itself the *essential* crime, and can never become its own vindication.

But it is even so. The evil *does* lie too deep for the reach of human remedies. Yet a remedy there is, and an effectual one. It is here—"*I will sprinkle clean water upon you, and ye shall be*

* Job viii. 1. † Rom. viii. 7.

clean ; *from all your filthiness, and from all your idols will I cleanse you. A* NEW HEART *also will I* GIVE *you, and a* NEW SPIRIT *will I* PUT *within you : And I will* TAKE AWAY *the* STONY HEART *out of your flesh ;* and I *will* GIVE *you an* HEART OF FLESH. *And I will* PUT MY SPIRIT WITHIN YOU, *and* CAUSE *you to walk in my statutes ; and ye shall keep my judgments and do them.** Try *this* expedient : Go, with thy " filthiness" and thine " idols :" Go, with thy " stony heart" and thy perverse spirit, which are thy real inability, to God upon the *throne of grace ;* spread out before him his " exceeding great and precious promise," importune him as the hearer of prayer, in the name of JESUS, for the accomplishment of it to thyself—wait for his mercy : it is worth waiting for—and remember his word ; *Therefore will the Lord wait, that he may be* GRACIOUS UNTO YOU; *and therefore will he be exalted that he* MAY HAVE MERCY *upon you : for the Lord is a God of judgment ; blessed are all they that wait for him.*†

The *rights* and *duties* of the children of believing parents, arising out of their relation to the church, is only part of our second result, as they are mutual, let us now turn the question and view it in its relation to the rights and *duties* of the *Christian church toward such children.*

A right to provide for the proper education of their youth, has always been claimed, and exer-

---

* Ezek. xxxvi. 25—27.   † Is. xxx. 18.

cised in some form or other, by every civilized community. It is, indeed, inherent in the very nature of human society; as it springs out of that great, universal, and essential principle of man—self-preservation. The risen generation, is, for the most part, fixed. Their habits are formed, their characters settled, and what is to be expected from them may be ascertained with sufficient exactness for the principal purposes of life. Not so with the rising race. No sagacity can foretell what characters shall be developed, or what parts performed, by these boys and girls who throng our streets, and sport in our fields. In their tender breasts are concealed the germs, in their little hands are lodged the weapons, of a nation's overthrow or glory. Would it not, then, be madness; would it not be a sort of political suicide, for the commonwealth to be unconcerned what direction their infant powers shall take; or into what habits their budding affections shall ripen? Or will it be disputed, that the civil authority has a *right* to take care, by a paternal interference, on behalf of the children, that the next generation shall not prostrate in an hour, whatever has been consecrated to truth, to virtue, and to happiness, by the generations that are past?

If this is the common privilege of human nature, on what principle shall it be denied to the church of God? Spiritual in her character, furnished with

every light to guide the understanding; and every
precept to mould the heart—possessing whatever
is fearful to deter from sin, and whatever is sweet
and alluring to win to God and holiness, how is it
possible that she can have no *right* to bring these
her advantages to bear upon the youth committed
to her trust ? Why were they thus committed?
How shall she deserve the name of the spouse of
Christ, if she endeavour not to bring up her own
children in his " nurture and admonition ?" Admitting the children of believing parents to be her
members, the right to instruct and watch over
them, is a matter of course. For it is a solecism
and an absurdity to talk of a society which has
no authority over its own members. And when
we establish the *right*, we establish also the *duty*.
The power is given to be employed. It is a talent
for which the master will demand an account. If
he has authorized his church to take charge of
the children within her pale, she is responsible for
the manner in which she acquits herself of the
trust. How is this to be done?

1st. All baptized children, (whom by their baptism she acknowledges to be a part of her care,)
are to be instructed by her authority, and under
her eye.

There is a domestic training which it is her
business to see that parents give their children.
But she has an interest in these children altoge-

ther her own. Her ministers, or official catechists, are, in her name, to instill into them, the principles of the Christian religion, *over and above their tuition at home;* and whether their parents be faithful to them or not. A child is not to be turned off, and left a prey to destruction, because its parents do not shrink from the crime of " blood-guiltiness," even guiltiness of the blood of their own offspring. Means are, therefore, to be used, that *all* the children of a congregation attend *public* instruction in the doctrines and duties of religion, as an *ordinance of Christ;* and to have the sense of their subjection to his ordinances incorporated with their earliest habits of thinking. No church can neglect this care without suffering: no church has ever fostered it without abundant recompense. The most intelligent, sober, staid, active Christians, are usually those who have grown up under the operation of this gentle but efficient discipline.

2d. The church is to inspect the *conduct* of her youth.

I do not mean that she is to encourage hawkers of scandal, nor to entertain legions of spies, for their benefit. Not that she is to put on that dismal visage which petrifies the juvenile heart; nor to indulge that morose inquisition which arraigns, as a crime, every burst of juvenile cheerfulness. It is as much a part of God's *natural* constitution that youth should be sprightly, as that age should be grave. To reduce to one size and one quality, all the decencies of life in all its periods, is the attribute of zeal which never discriminates, of severity which never learns, or of Pharisaism which finds a righteousness in reprobating enjoyments which it cannot share.

But, after every proper allowance and precaution, there is left a large field of juvenile conduct for the eye of the church to explore. Both in affirming the principles of rectitude, and in resisting the principles of evil, she may and she ought to do much for her youth.

If a child be exemplary in filial or fraternal affection; pure in behaviour among others; diligent in learning the precious truths of revelation; reverential towards the ordinances of public and private worship; fearful of sinning against God; it is no small encouragement to have these excellencies observed, cherished, and honoured, by those who bear rule in the church. Timidity subsides; bashfulness is attempered into modesty; the ductile inclination grows into consistent purpose; and thus " little ones" are brought to Jesus Christ, and prepared for occupying, in due season, the places of those whose gray hairs announce the approach of that hour in which they are to be numbered with them who have died in faith.

On the other hand, can any reflecting person doubt, that the seasonable interposition of the

church of God, might save many a youth from
falling a victim to his own depravity, or to the depravity of others? Why should a doubt be entertained on the subject? Is the experiment fairly
tried? Are the churches in the habit of throwing
themselves in between ruin and the youth who
have not openly professed religion? Do parents,
on the failure of domestic admonition, *ever* resort
to this remedy? Ought they not to do it? Why
should a tender and solemn remonstrance, in the
name of the living God, the Creator and the Judge
of all, be without its influence in recovering an
unpractised sinner from the errour of the wicked?
Why should not an *authoritative* expostulation, on
the part of the church of God, brought home to
individual feeling, have some effect, as a rational
means, in prevailing with the young to consider
their obligation to recognize the vows made over
them in their baptism? There are more troublesome consciences on this point, among our youth,
than we, perhaps, imagine. Why should they not
be told, that continuance in carelessness, or abandonment to iniquity, will compel the church of
God to disown them, and to rank them with those
concerning whom she has no promises to plead?
Let it not be said that " the state of religious society forbids such an interference—that parents
and children would spurn at it as an encroach-
ment upon their liberty—and that instead of

gaining our youth, it would drive them, **at once,** into the camp of the profane ;"—at least, let not these things be said without *facts* to support them. They are the suggestions of fear, unsanctioned by experience. No doubt, in the decayed state of Christian order, much prudence is necessary for its revival : but the necessity of prudence cannot excuse inaction. It is very possible, also, that some young saints would " kick against the pricks." But the same objection lies against the faithful preaching of the word ; and against the impartial use of discipline toward professors. There are weighty reasons why a judicious extension of church authority to baptised youth in general, would not be so fruitless and despicable as some suppose.

First, The mere power of *opinion* which it would employ, could not be easily resisted. It is to be remembered, that a very little quantity of opinion goes a great way with all minds which have not yet acquired self-stability ; and *such* opinion as the Christian church can at all times command, no man living *can* disregard with impunity.

Secondly, In many instances, this interference would combine with domestic precept and example ; and how far their united forces would go, nothing but the event is entitled to pronounce.

Thirdly, Dissolute as the world is, and disposed as multitudes are to scoff at every thing which bears the image and superscription of Jesus Christ, it will be no recommendation even with thoughtless people, that a young person fled away from the voice of kindly instruction; much less that he was thrust out on account of his vices. Some there are, who, to serve the present hour, would applaud his spirit; and, on the first disagreement, would upbraid him with his disgrace. It is not in human nature to stand easily under an excommunication of *any sort.* Exclusion, for faults, from any decent society, is, and ever will be, a stigma. Whoever disbelieves it, has only to try.

Fourthly, The providence of our Lord Jesus Christ, and his control over the hearts and affairs of men, are especially to be regarded. Perhaps no instance can be shown of contempt upon the discipline of his house not being followed, sooner or later, with most disastrous consequences to the offender. He has promised to own, support, and vindicate it, as solemnly as he ever promised to bless the gospel of his grace. If more stress were laid upon *his* agency in rendering effectual his own institutions; we should both discharge our duty more exactly, and see it crowned with greater success. Let the churches *begin* to look after their youth—let them commit their efforts to their master's faithfulness. It will be time enough to complain when he " leaves himself without a witness."

3d. There is a particular class of children to whom the church owes a duty which she too frequently neglects—I mean *orphans.*

Godly parents die; and their little ones are scattered. Scattered, indeed, they often must be, but forgotten they ought not to be. They are often permitted to be placed in families where they can reap no religious benefit. All responsibility for them seems to be thrown away, and given to the winds with the last breath of their father or mother. Thus abandoned by the church, which ought to be to them in God's stead, and when their father and their mother forsake them, to take them up, they are in danger of being lost in this world, and in the world to come. I speak immediately of those who have no private dependence but the bounty of strangers. Guilt in this matter, there certainly is, and the sooner we arise to shake it out of our skirts, the better will it be for ourselves, and our *own* children.

Beside the conclusions which we have drawn from the general Constitution of the Church of God, relative to Christian communion, and the rights and duties mutually subsisting between the Church and her infant members, there is a

Third result relative to her officers; especially those who labour in the word and doctrine. It is this : *They are* PRIMARILY *the property of the* CHURCH CATHOLIC ; *and only in a* SECONDARY *and*

SUBORDINATE *sense, the property of a particular congregation.*

Throughout the christianized world, it has always been customary, in a greater or less degree,
to remove ministers of the gospel from one pastoral
charge to another, or to liberate them from pastoral ties altogether, that they might promote, in a
different form, the interests of the Christian cause.
For very obvious reasons, these removals happen
most frequently to men of talents. Nor is there a
single thing which creates more uneasiness and
heart-burning. It is perfectly natural. For neither
individuals nor societies are fond of parting with
what they consider a treasure. Able, faithful, discreet ministers, are a rare blessing; and it would
say little for the understanding, and less for the
religion, of any Church which should lightly re-
linquish it. We must further admit, that a wan-
ton disruption of the pastoral ties is foolish, un-
warrantable, and extensively pernicious.

Still the question of its propriety must be tried,
not by examples of its abuse, nor by its unpopula-
rity, but by the *principles* on which it is founded,
This cannot be done, without examining the nature of the claim which a particular congregation
has to her minister.

The pastoral connexion is commonly compared
to a matrimonial connexion; which, being for

life, the popular inference is, that the pastoral connexion also is for life.

This proves nothing, except the facility with which most people impose upon themselves by sounds and similes. A simile is no argument. And the simile of a man and his wife, to denote a pastor and his congregation, is peculiarly unhappy. If it is to prescribe the duration of their union, it must also regulate the discharge of their duties. Now, as married persons must confine their matrimonial intercourse to themselves, not allowing a participation in it to any other, this simile, working up the ministerial relation into a sort of pastoral matrimony, would render it absolutely unlawful in a minister to hold religious communion with any other people, and in his people to hold religious communion with any other minister. Nor, if a minister's just maintenance should grow inconvenient to a people's finances, or he should fall into disfavour, even without any charge of misconduct, would they think it sound reasoning to turn upon them with their own simile, and say, " A minister and his people are as husband and wife. A wife takes her husband for better for worse; so did you take your minister; and as you took him you must keep him. The plea of poverty or disgust is of no avail; a woman is not to quit her husband whenever she thinks that he spends too much of the fortune she brought him; nor is she to run away from him merely because she does not like him any longer, or has a fancy for some one else. This is no better than downright adultery : and such is the behaviour of a congregation, who has grown tired of a minister, and wishes to get rid of him." It would be very hard to persuade a congregation that this is correct reasoning ; and yet it is exactly such reasoning as we hear every day against the removal of a minister, grounded on the notion of something like a marriage covenant between him and his charge. The reasoning proceeds from feelings pretty general among men, prompting them to prefer a bargain which shall be all on one side, and that side their own. They wish to have the whole comfort without risk of privations on the one hand, or of irksome burdens on the other. It is perfectly equitable in their eyes, that a minister should leave them to better *their* situation ; but to leave them in order to better *his own*, is almost, if not altogether, an adulterous desertion ; and even if it be to forward upon a larger scale, and with more efficacy, the advantage of Christ's kingdom, his authoritative removal is little, if at all, less than robbery !

But let us be just. They are not the people only who adopt this preposterous reasoning. Ministers have too frequently fallen into the same errour ; and, in some instances, they have exactly reversed the popular conclusions; stating it as good and wholesome doctrine, that a minister should have it in his power to retain his cure as long as he pleases; and to resign it when he pleases; but should by no means be subject to removal when the people wish it. Thus, in their turn, making the bargain all on their own side. This is paltry work : It is, on both sides, a calculation fit only for sharpers. In so far as it arises from honest opinion, it springs out of a radical mistake, which is to be rectified by considering how the unity of the visible church affects ministerial character and labours.

The mistake is this: that " a minister and his congregation possess each other, if I may so word it, in a mutual fee simple—that they have an exclusive and absolute right to each other;" whereas no such possession, no such right does, or can, exist.

Our Lord Jesus Christ, when he " ascended up on high, leading captivity captive, gave gifts unto men. And he gave some," (i. e. some whom he gave were,) " apostles; and some, prophets; and some, evangelists; and some, pastors and teachers; for the perfecting of the saints; for the work of the ministry; for the edifying of the body of Christ." Eph. iv.

Here ministers of the gospel are said to be Christ's ascension-gift to his church ! But what church ? Certainly not a particular congregation, for the gift includes ministers who never *could be* confined to so limited a charge. No one particular congregation ; no, nor any section of Christians, though containing *many* congregations, could appropriate to themselves the labours of an apostle, or an evangelist. These were, beyond all contradiction, officers of the church catholic, or of the church visible.* But it is to the same church that Christ has given the *ordinary* ministry, " pastors and teachers." They are included in one and the same gift. Therefore, a minister belongs primarily and immediately to the church catholic ; and only *mediately*, that is, through the medium of the church catholic, is assigned to a particular congregation. It is, of course, *her* province and duty to determine how, and where, he shall be employed. The only rule of judgment is, *the greatest amount of benefit which may accrue from his services to the interests of the Redeemer's kingdom.* The determination of this point must be confided to such a portion of the church catholic, assembled in judicatory, (since it is impossible for the whole to meet,) as shall secure, according to human probabilities, a wise and impartial decision. To lodge such a power in the hands of a particular congregation, would be manifestly improper ;

See page 1—26.

for it would not only make one set of men the
judges in their own case, and in their neighbour's
too, but would subject the great interests of the
church of God to the control of persons unfur-
nished with sufficient information, often impas-
sioned, always prepossessed ; and, therefore, incapable of "judging righteous judgment." Mistakes, and improprieties will, no doubt, occur, be
the power where it may : because perfection is to
be found no where. Yet, when a question is to
be tried before a court composed of representa-
tives from several particular churches, having much
more ability, and better opportunities of informing
themselves, than the mass of any congregation can
have : being also free from that selfish bias to
which the best minds and hearts are liable from
calculations directly affecting themselves, it is in
as fair a way of being decided well, as the imperfection of man admits. When such a court, then,
fixes the pastoral relation between a minister and
a congregation, it does not surrender him up absolutely to them ; nor wed them to each other for
life. It places him there, because it believes that
his labours there will be, upon the whole, most
useful to the church at large. And the principle
which regulates the formation, must also regulate
the continuance, of his pastoral relations. He is
to remain so long as the church of God shall gain
more by his continuance than by his removal, and

no longer. Whenever it shall clearly appear that his labours may be turned to better account by his removal than by his continuance, he ought to be removed: not, however, at his own discretion, or the discretion of his people, but upon the same careful examination by the church representative, as preceded his first settlement. We repeat, that it would be unreasonable and unrighteous, to let an individual or a congregation possess the power of sacrificing to their narrow gratification, the interest of the Christian community. Ministers, then, must be in that situation which shall render their labours of the greatest utility. They are ordinarily joined to parochial charges; because this, upon the whole, is the best practical system; and not because their charges have an exclusive property in them. The claims of the church at large, always supersede the claims of any particular part; so that whatever be the attachment of a people to their minister, or of a minister to his people, when the *general* claim is set up, their particular feelings must give way; and that upon this self-evident truth, that the whole is greater than a part. Pursuing the same reasoning, we perceive, that whether a minister shall have a congregation or not, is a question of secondary importance; and is to be answered by a prudent consideration of the previous question,—whether he is likely to be more extensively useful with or without a congregation?

That removals from charges where men are beloved and useful, ought not to be rash; ought not to take place, without the most solid reasons; ought, in all cases, to be managed with circumspection and with dignity; that the very uneasiness excited by such removals, ought to be weighed in the balances among the strong reasons against them are dictates of common sense and equity; and no wise judicatory will ever disregard them. But that the *principle* is sound—that a minister may *lawfully* be removed from one charge to another; or from one species of labour to another, cannot be controverted, without tearing up the foundations of the whole church of God.

Finally. A very important result from the foregoing discussions concerning the nature of the church is, that *no form of church government can be scriptural, which is not adapted to this broad and master-principle, that the visible church is* ONE.

Her external organization must be such as shall show her to the world, as *a living body*, according to the apostle's figure. Eph. iv. 12. 16. She must, therefore, have principles, and means, of common action. The whole must control the parts—She must have a power of self-preservation, which includes,

1. A power of commanding the agency of any particular member :
2. A power of combining the agency of *all* her members :
3. A power of providing for her nourishment and health :
4. A power of expelling impurities and corruptions.

These things are essential to her organization according to the description given of her in the word of God. We may have occasion to illustrate them more particularly hereafter ; we close, at present, with one remark—that a number of particular churches not united in mutual dependence, and not furnished with a principle of living efficiency in one common system, so as to bring the strength of the whole to operate in any part, or through all the parts collectively, as occasion may require, no more resemble the visible church of Christ, than the limbs of the human body, dissevered, and not " fitly joined together, and compacted by that which every joint supplieth, according to the effectual working in the measure of every part," resemble a healthy man.

CHURCH OF GOD.

No. VIII.

Officers.

A COMMUNITY so large, and yet so compact; formed, preserved, and perpetuated with so much care; directed to so high an end; and furnished with principles of such universal application, as we have proved the church of God to be, requires a suitable regimen. God is the God of order: no order can be kept up any where without government; and no government can exist without officers to administer it. Our next inquiry, therefore, relates to the *officers* whom Christ hath appointed.

In the Apostolical church were the following : viz.

    1. APOSTLES,—1 Cor. xii. 28. Eph. iv. 11.
    2. PROPHETS,—Rom. xii. 6. 1 Cor. xii. 28
                 Eph. iv. 11.
    3. EVANGELISTS,—Eph. iv. 11.

4. Pastors and teachers,—*Ibid.* Acts xiii. 1.

who *ruled,*——

who also *laboured in word and doctrine,*—— } 1 Tim. v. 17.

5. Elders, who " ruled" *without* " labouring in word and doctrine,"——*Ibid.*

6. Deacons,——Acts vi. 1—6. 1. Tim. iii. 8.

It is evident that the great object of all these offices was the religious education of the world. We mean that they were intended to instruct mankind in the knowledge of divine truth ; to inspire them with pure principles and spiritual affections; to form their individual and social habits to practical holiness, and moral order; in one word, to render them " meet for the inheritance of the saints in light."

It is also evident, that some of these offices were only temporary. Which of them were designed to be permanent, and in what form, is an inquiry which we must postpone till we shall have settled a previous question.

It has been, and still is, a received belief among almost all who profess Christianity, that the Redeemer has instituted a regular ministry to be perpetuated in an order of men specially set apart and commissioned by his authority, for the purpose of inculcating the doctrines and duties of Christianity ; and that no man may lawfully enter upon its functions without an official warrant from them who are themselves already in office.

Others contend that this whole system is of human origin; is founded either in ignorance or in fraud; and militates directly against the nature and privileges of the Christian church.

Others again, attempt a middle course; allowing the general principle of a ministry, but leaving the application of it at large; and conceiving the exercise of gifts with the approbation of the *church*, that is, a number of professing Christians met together for public worship, to be a valid and sufficient call.

To clear up this matter, let us consider,

1. What the scriptures have determined concerning the *fact* in dispute : and

2. What are the uses, qualifications, and mode of preserving, a standing ministry.

1. As to the *fact*. These things are worthy of regard.

1st. It is undeniable, that from the time God set up his church in her organized form, (and even before,) until the Christian dispensation, there was an order of men consecrated, by his own appointment, to the exclusive work of directing her worship, and presiding over her interests: insomuch that no man, but one of themselves, not even a crowned head, might meddle with their functions; nor undertake, in any way, to be a

public teacher of religion, without an immediate
call from heaven attested by miraculous evidence.

2d. The ancient prophets, " who spake as they
were moved by the Holy Ghost," foretold that the
same principle should be acted upon in the days of
the Messiah. Thus in Isa. lxvi. 21. *I will also take
of them for* PRIESTS *and for* LEVITES, *saith* JEHO-
VAH—and Dan. xiii. 3. *They that be wise shall
shine as the brightness of the firmament, and they that
turn many to righteousness, as the stars for ever and
ever.* The word rendered " wise," signifies teachers," whose business, and, according as they are
blessed of God, whose happiness, it is to turn men
unto righteousness. Our Lord himself has used
the term in the same sense, as indeed it was a
very common signification among the people of
the East: *Behold I send you prophets, and* WISE MEN,
and scribes. Matt. xxiii. 34. The force of the argument is, that these predictions contemplate events
which were to take place in the Christian economy ; and without which they could not be fulfilled.
The passage from Isaiah refers to the " new hea-
vens and the new earth" which the Lord should
make : consequently, to New Testament times :
And not only so, but to their most illustrious period—the restoration of the Jews, and the glory
of the latter day. " Priests and Levites," to perform services similar to those under the old economy, there can be none ; because the end of

those services being accomplished, their further continuance is impossible; and the economy itself has vanished away. Yet the prediction and the promise must be fulfilled: and can mean nothing less than this, that as the Priests and the Levites were appointed of God to minister·in holy things during the former dispensation, and in a manner suited to its peculiar character; so there should be appointed of God, under the new dispensation, a ministry corresponding to its peculiar character; which ministry should flourish even in those days when the most copious effusions of the divine Spirit should seem to render it the least necessary. And this is a full answer to the objection brought from the promise that all Zion's *children shall be taught of God—and they shall teach no more every man his neighbour, and every man his brother, saying,* " *know the Lord :" for they shall all know me from the least of them unto the greatest of them, saith the Lord.* Jer. xxxi. 34.

We say that an objection drawn from such passages against a Christian ministry, as regular and exclusive as the ministry of the Levitical Law, is of no weight:

For in the *first*, place, they are not more full and explicit than those passages which promise such a ministry: and as both are true, no interpretation can be admitted of one, which shall contradict the other.

Secondly, If the objection is well-founded, it sweeps away not only a standing ministry; but all religious instruction in every shape: prohibiting even parents to " bring up their children in the nurture and admonition of the Lord ;" and putting under a bushel the very light of the " gifted brethren"—which would be rather lamentable.

Thirdly, There is the most perfect consistency between a great diffusion of religious light, and great use of religious teachers. We find, by experience, that the most enlightened Christians do most honour and value an enlightened ministry. The ignorant, and the vain are most ready to suppose that they need no instruction. *Give instruction to a wise man, and he will be yet wiser; teach a just man, and he will increase in learning*, (Prov. ix. 9.) *But, seest thou a man wise in his own conceit? there is more hope of a fool than of him*, (xxvi. 12.) The "principalities and powers in heavenly places," were no novices in the knowledge of God. But when they wished to obtain still larger views of his " manifold wisdom." they did not blush to take a lesson from the lips of Paul, (Eph. iii. 10.)

There is no difficulty in the appellation of " Priests and Levites ;" seeing it was customary with the prophets to speak of New Testament blessings in Old Testament style ; and not practicable for them to use any other, and be sufficiently intelligible.

3d. Our Lord Jesus Christ delivered their commission to his apostles in terms which necessarily imply a perpetual and regularly successive ministry. *Go ye, and* TEACH ALL NATIONS, *baptizing them in the name of the Father, and of the Son, and of the Holy Ghost : Teaching them to observe all things whatsoever I have commanded you ; and, lo, I am with you* ALWAY, *even unto the* END OF THE WORLD, Matt. xxviii. 19.

That this command and promise though immediately addressed, were not limited, to the apostles, is so obvious as almost to shame an argument. But since we are sometimes required to prove that two and two make four, we remark,

First. That as the command is to teach all nations ; it must spread as far, and last as long as nations shall be found. It is therefore a command to make the Christian religion universal; and to perpetuate it from generation to generation.

Secondly. That as the Apostles were shortly to " put off their tabernacles," the command could not possibly be fulfilled by them. It runs parallel with the existence of nations. It must, therefore, be executed by others, in every age, who are to carry on the work which the apostles begun; and who, by the very terms of the commandment, are identified with them in the general spirit of their commission, which is, to preach the doctrines,

enforce the precepts, and administer the ordinances, of Jesus Christ.

Thirdly. That the promise, " I am with you alway, even unto the end of the world," cannot without palpable absurdity, be restricted to the persons, nor to the days of the Apostles. Closely
rendered it is, " I am with you always, even until
the *consummation of the age,*" i. e. " dispensation."*
But what age ? what dispensation ? Either the
Jewish, or the Christian.

Not the Jewish, certainly. It would be very
strange if the grace of the Redeemer's promise
should abide with his apostles till the end of the
old dispensation, and run out exactly at the moment when it was wanted for the new one. The
" world," therefore, is that " world" which Paul
calls " the world to come," (Heb. ii. 5.) i. e. the
Christian dispensation. " I have just introduced
it," says the master, " and I will be with you to
the close of it." The promise, then, as well as the
precept, reaches to the end of time ; and, like the
precept, embraces a successive ministry to whom
our Lord Jesus has engaged the continuance of
his gracious presence.

4th. The Apostles themselves acted upon the
principle of a perpetual ministry. " They ordained Presbyters in every church," (Acts xiv. 23.)
Paul has left, in his epistles to Timothy and Titus,

* Ἐως της συντελειας του αιωνος.

as a part of the rule of faith and practice, particular directions for the choice of Bishops or Presbyters and deacons: And in his epistle to the Hebrews, (ch. xiii. 17.) he charges these widely scattered disciples, to obey their spiritual rulers, under this precise idea that they *watch*, says he, *for your souls as they that must give account.*

5th. The New Testament abounds with predictions and warnings of *apostacy* in the ministers of religion; which of course, implies the *continuance* of a ministry.

6th. The book of Revelation expressly recognizes the diffusion of the Gospel, in times yet to come, by the instrumentality of a public ministry, (ch. xiv. 6.)

Since, therefore, the Head of the church instituted a regular ministry in his church thousands of years ago—since he directed his prophets to foretell its existence under the new dispensation—since he gave to his apostles a commission which necessarily supposes its perpetuity—since these apostles themselves acted upon that principle in erecting churches—since the rule of faith has given instructions to guide its application—since the prophetic spirit in the last of the apostles has uttered oracles which are founded upon it—no conclusion is more safe and irrefragable than this; that a regular, standing ministry is an essential constituent of the church of God.

This point settled, that our Lord Jesus Christ has instituted a ministry which is to be coeval with his church, we now proceed

2. To consider the uses, qualifications, and mode of preserving, a standing ministry.

1st. Its *uses.*

The common sense of mankind, in all ages and countries, has taught them, that no system of religion can be maintained and perpetuated, without an order of religious teachers. Search the world over, and you shall not find a nation, civilized or savage, without such an order. The truth or falsehood of the religious system has no immediate connexion with this argument. It is founded upon a principle which includes the cardinal secret of human improvement—the *division of labour.* In other words, that to ensure excellence in any occupation whatever, it must be confined to a particular class of men, and these men must be confined to it. Set ten individuals to work at ten different species of industry, so that every one shall be employed by turns upon all the ten; let other ten work at the very same things, but distribute them so as that each of the ten shall have his appropriate employment, never intermeddling with the other nine; and two effects will follow—*First,* The produce of each particular species of industry will be incomparably better; and, *Secondly,* The aggregate produce of all will be incomparably greater, upon the second plan than upon the first. That is, the work performed in the ten branches of industry by ten men, each one being limited to a particular branch, will be incomparably superiour in quality and quantity, to the work performed by the same number of hands labouring promiscuously in all the branches. Whoever disputes this position, has yet to learn the first letter in the alphabet of human experience. Apply this to the church of God. The religious cultivation of a people upon the principles of revelation, furnishes matter not only for a *separate* calling; but for a calling which requires *subdivision*.

The rules of faith and duty are comprised in a miscellaneous volume, the different parts of which are to be studied, compared, explained, enforced. This is not the work of a novice ; of an occasional exhorter; of one who spends six days of the week in a secular employment ; and comes forth on the sabbath to vent his babblings under the name of preaching. Talent, learning, and labour, have found the week short enough for the right preparation of a people's spiritual food, and the discharge of other ministerial functions. In proportion as intellect is strong, knowledge deep, and the habit of application vigorous, is a sense of the ministerial trust impressive and awful. Feebleness of mind, and the conceit of ignorance,

make it sit light upon the heart, and frustrate
some of its noblest effects.

Were we not accustomed to absurdities, we
should think it unaccountable, that, while the education of children is an exclusive occupation, the
education and direction of children and men both,
should ever be merely an incidental matter ; and
be left to the chance-medley of a fugitive hour!
Had Christianity set out upon this maxim, she had
never reached the age of one hundred years. Her
divine head did not commit her, for a single day,
to such irregular and incompetent guidance.
Those things which, in later times, are the fruit of
patient and painful investigation, were, at the beginning of her career, in the East, open to every
eye and familiar to every mind. Yet her teachers
were a separate order, as the very face of her history in the New Testament shows. If Timothy,
who was an extraordinary officer, a native of those
regions from which the scriptural allusions and
illustrations are taken ; a disciple, too, of an inspired master, was enjoined to " *give himself to
reading*, to exhortation, to doctrine ;" if he was not
to neglect, but to stir up the " gift which was in
him, which was given him by prophecy, with the
laying on of the hands of the Presbytery"—If he
was to meditate upon these things ; to give himself *wholly* to them ; that his *profiting* might appear to all ;" how can equal diligence and appli-

cation be dispensed with in others who have to encounter much greater difficulties without the same advantage? How dare men, not possessing the hundredth part of the information necessary to elucidate a single chapter of the Bible, which happens to contain matter beyond the simplest rudiments of Christianity, how do they *dare*, under such circumstances, to ascend the pulpit as expounders of " the oracles of the living God ?" If " the priest's lips must keep knowledge, because he is the messenger of the Lord of Hosts," how shall the crude and undisciplined mind " bring forth things new and old ?" It is not possible; the constitution of God's world forbids, that a man who is busied six days out of seven, in mechanical, commercial, or other secular toil, should have his intellect *trained* to the immensely important and comprehensive duty of instructing his fellowmen in the will of God, and the science of happiness. If the diffusion of religious light; if the formation of the moral habits of a community; if the prevention and suppression of errour and vice; if the consolation of the afflicted; if the administration of ordinances designed of God as means of eternal life, do not demand an entire devotedness of those to whom they are intrusted, nothing can.

It is vain and foolish to dissemble facts. All sound exposition of the scriptures; i. e. all the

pure and steady light of truth which shines in the
churches, has been the work of men thus devoted.
The discourses of others are, for the most part,
mere shreds pilfered from the webs woven by that
industry, learning, and talent, which they affect
to undervalue. That usurpation of the sacred
office, termed *lay-preaching*, now grown so common, cannot fail, unless a miracle should invert
the course of nature, to degrade, and if it become
general, to destroy, the ministry of reconciliation.
The enemy could desire nothing more noxious to
Christianity, than gradually to expel all cultivated
talent from her pulpits; and to throw her interests into the hands of men self-approved, and self-
sent. There is, indeed, an apology, which, though
insufficient, cannot be denied to have a foundation. Shrewd men, even in vulgar life, hear
preachers, who, in the cant prase, have been *regularly bred*, utter very small discourse; confine
their lucubrations to a few plain points, repeat the
same things in the same way, and that none of
the best, until every person of a tolerably retentive
memory, can tell pretty nearly beforehand, what
" entertainment" is to be expected. With such
facts habitually before them, they learn to imagine that the ministry is no mighty affair; they
say, and they say truly, that " they can preach as
well themselves ;" and the next step is *to try*. The
people perceive no great superiority or inferiority;

and why should they maintain a man for giving them instruction of no better quality, than they can get for little or nothing? All this is natural; and more, it is reasonable. Why, indeed? Let us not pretend to dispute what the world knows to be true. Let us not shut our eyes upon our own disgrace, and the ruin of the Christian cause.

Pudet hæc opprobria! We have ample ground for humiliation. There are many, many " regularly bred" clergy, who are much fitter to make shoes, or buttons, or baskets, than to make sermons. No disrespect to any branch of mechanical industry; but every thing in its place. No men can be more out of place, than multitudes who are in the ministry. It was a sad mistake which caused them to stray into the pulpit. How has this happened? By what fatal perversion has the province of *instructing* mankind in things pertaining to God and to eternity, fallen so frequently into the hands of the ignorant and stupid? And why, when young men, neither stupid nor ignorant, enter upon it, does the progress of their ministry so little correspond with its original promise?

There are two prominent reasons.

(1.) The miserable provision for their temporal support.

When men consecrate themselves to the religious weal of a people, and do, by that act, forego the opportunities open to all others, of providing

for themselves and their families, a competent
maintenance is the least remuneration which they
have a right to claim.   It is the dictate of common sense, common justice, and common huma-
nity.   It is also the express commandment of our
Lord Jesus Christ.   But, notwithstanding these
considerations, the ministry is little better than a
starving profession. Not one man in twenty, were
he compelled to live upon the salary allowed by
his congregation, could escape from beggary and
rags.   The certain effect is, on the one hand, to
deter young men of respectable talents from the
•ministry altogether ; and, on the other, to discour-
age, depress and finally to ruin those who are in
it already.

That degree of talent which fits one, so far as
intellectual endowments go, for a useful minister
of the Gospel, is much rarer than many seem to
imagine; and, humanly speaking, has its temporal
prosperity in its own power. When other pursuits
invite by the promise of not only a maintenance,
but of gain, and even of opulence, it is idle, it is
unreasonable, to hope that youth of talents, without fortune, whatever be their piety, will serve the
church of God at the expense of devoting themselves to infallible penury, and all the wretchedness
which belongs to it.   They may desire, they may
wish; and, in some instances, from that simplicity
which never calculates or which flatters itself that

something favourable " will turn up," they may venture : but in general, they must turn away with a sigh from the employment which, of all others, their hearts most long after. Let us not hear of self-denial, spiritual-mindedness, and a heroic indifference to worldly things, as characteristic of the true minister of Christ. Self-denial does not mean starving. The spirituality of the father will not stop the cravings of his children when they cry for food; nor is there any heroism in preferring tatters and a hovel to decent clothing and lodging, when they may be had. It is very convenient, no doubt, for men who are adding house to house, field to field, thousand to thousand, to harangue, in a religious style, on the necessity of a minister's imitating his master, " who had not where to lay his head;" when the practical inference from all this is in favour of their own pockets. They are wonderfully concerned for spirituality and self-denial to be practised by their ministers; but as to their *own* share of these virtues; as to *their* parting with a pittance of *their* pelf to render him comfortable—why—that is another affair. It is one of the most wicked forms of hypocrisy to plead for the cultivation of a minister's heavenly-mindedness, by way of an apology for cheating him out of his bread. The sin of the neglect complained of is not equally gross in all. In some it proceeds from thoughtlessness; in others from incapacity to make a right estimate ; but in most, it is the fruit of downright covetousness. There has been, on this subject, an absurd squeamishness in those whom the Lord has authorized to " live by the gospel." They have borne, and forborne ; they have submitted to every species of sacrifice rather than disoblige their people ; and their only reward has been an accumulation of injuries and cold-blooded contempt. It is time for them to claim their due in a modest, but manly tone ; and throw the fearful responsibility of expelling an enlightened ministry from the church upon those who are able, but not willing, to support it honour-ably. We say an " enlightened" ministry. For we have no conception that niggardly provision will soon strip her of every thing in the shape of a minister. You cannot place the pecuniary recompense so low, as that it shall not be an object for somebody. Fix your salaries at 50 dollars a-year, and you shall not want candidates. But then they will be *fifty-dollar-men.* All genius, all learning, all high character, all capacity for exten-sive usefulness, will be swept away ; and rudeness, ignorance, impudence, and vulgarity, will become the religious directors of the nation. The man is blind who does not see matters fast hastening to this issue in the United States.

In the mean time, such ministers as are better qualified for their stations, are not only decreasing

in proportion to the population, but with few ex-
ceptions, are prohibited from cultivating the powers which they possess.   Remote from literary society; without libraries; without leisure to use
what books they have; distracted with anxiety
for their immediate subsistence; doomed to the
plough or some other secular business, to keep
themselves fed and clothed, their intellect becomes
enfeebled; their acquisitions are dissipated; their
ministry grows barren; their people indifferent;
and the solid interests of Christianity are gradually, but effectually, undermined.   Let the churches
be warned.   They have long slept on the edge of
a precipice; the ground is caving in below them;
and still they are not aware.   Not a place of any
importance is to be filled without the utmost difficulty.   The search must be made from Dan to
Beersheeba; often, very often, unsuccessfully; and
when successful it is only enriching one church by
the robbery of another.   The population of our
country is increasing with unexampled rapidity;
very incompetent means are used to furnish an efficient ministry; and the people themselves are
throwing the most fatal discouragement in the
way.   All denominations seem to be engaged in a
practical conspiracy to starve Christianity out of
the land.   Let them tremble at their deeds; let
their loins be loosed, and their knees smite to-

gether, at the bare possibility that they MAY SUCCEED.

But it is not the people only who are in fault; for,

(2.) Much of the guilt of decayed Christianity lies at the doors of the ministers and judicatories of the church.

It is not *arguing* for the divine right of a stated ministry; it is not boasting about the excellence of " our church ;" it is not lamenting over the supineness of the.public, that will cure the evil.   It is the *procuring a ministry which shall render attendance upon their ministrations the interest of both the understanding and the heart.*   Without this, every effort is vain: and this belongs to Christian judicatories.   Let the world see and feel that there is an immense superiority of the regular over an irregular ministry, and there will be no more lay-preaching ; nor so much difficulty in getting a decent support.   But it cannot be concealed, that little as congregations give, they often give to the uttermost farthing, " for value received."   The mischief is, that the rule of abridgment becomes general, and the " workman who needeth not to be ashamed," must share the fate of him who is no workman at all.   Ministers have themselves to blame for much of this evil.   They have lowered the standard of ministerial qualifications.   They usher into their high office men who have neither head nor hands for any thing else. The apostolic directions, (in 1 Tim. 3.) are almost totally disregarded. Instead of " laying their hands suddenly on no man," they have been too much in the habit of laying hands upon every one they can find— novice or no novice—fit to teach or unfit—able to govern or unable ; all are accepted—nothing, or next to nothing, is refused. An absurd tenderness ; a fear of hurting the feelings of a young man or of his friends ; an infatuated haste to meet " the wants of the churches ;" has poured fourth a stream of ignorance and incapacity, which now threatens to sweep away the harvest it was designed to water. In the degradation of the pulpit ; in the butchery of the scriptures ; in the defaced beauty, and tottering pillars of the Christian fabric, is to be seen the reward of timid indulgence and chimerical hope. If the ministry, as a *public order*, is to regain its credit, its own mismanagement must be radically cured.

CHURCH OF GOD.

No. IX.

Ministry.—Qualifications.

THE *uses* of the Christian ministry, which was our first point, are, in several respects, so blended with its *qualifications*, which is our

2d point; that we cannot treat of the one without demonstrating the other.

It is the business of a Christian minister to instruct his people in what they are to believe concerning God, and what duty God requires of them. His *first* qualification, therefore, is *piety*.

We are sinners. The characteristic principle in the religion of sinners, that, without which it is absolutely worthless to them, is SALVATION by a REDEEMER. Remove this—take away the incarnation and atonement of the Lord Jesus Christ, give us any thing as the ground of our hope but *redemption through his blood, the forgiveness of sins according to the riches of his grace,* and there is no more Christianity. Now for men, calling themselves ministers of the Lord Jesus, to omit the cross where he *gave himself for us, an offering and a sacrifice to God of a sweet-smelling savour;* or to debase the doctrine of the cross so that it shall cease to be our exclusive trust for the pardon of our sin, is to lay the foundation of their ministry in treason to the Son of God. The doom of such unfaithful servants will be marked with peculiar severity and horrour. The Lord, the righteous judge, will require at their hands the blood of their fellow-sinners; and they shall perish with the perdition of those who *crucify him afresh, and put him to an open shame.*

Less fearful, indeed, but sufficient to strike our souls with alarm and dread, is the condition of one who preaches to others a gospel which he has not believed to his own salvation. What drudgery! what wearisomeness! to proclaim a Saviour whom he does not love! Display the precept and the penalty of the law, he may. Declare the doctrine of the cross, he may. Expound the Scriptures, in general, he may. Defend the truth against its adversaries, he may. But how *can* he give to every one his portion of meat in due season? How *can* he feed the sheep? How feed the lambs of Jesus Christ? How sympathize with the children of godly sorrow? How accompany the pilgrim through the valley of the shadow of death? How bind up the broken-hearted? How comfort

others with the consolation wherewith he himself
has been comforted of God ? For these, the most
benignant offices of the evangelical ministry, talent however great, and learning however pro-
found, if not sanctified by the grace, if not imbued
with the Spirit of Christ, are good for nothing. In
speculation a believer, in the efficient principles of
character an unbeliever, their possessor will pronounce his own judgment. Leaving to apostates
their whole pre-eminence of wo, he will find nothing enviable in his " portion among the hypocrites, where there shall be weeping, and wailing,
and gnashing of teeth."

Let those who are already in the ministry look
to their personal interest in the Lord Jesus Christ,
" lest, having preached the gospel to others, they
themselves be castaways." Let young men who
aspire to the sacred office, give all diligence, in
the first place, to " make their calling and election
sure." Let those to whom pertains the introduction of others into the ministry, endeavour, by all
such means as do not imply the judging of a man's
state without external evidence, to ascertain the
fruits of faith in their candidates for the pulpit.
Let parents and friends be extremely cautious in
destining a child, or a relative, at a very early
age, to the ministry of reconciliation. Let him
first, as a condemned sinner, " *receive* Christ Jesus
the Lord ;" and then, as a saved sinner, " *walk* in

him," before he " profess to testify the gospel of the grace of God."

But let us not be quoted as countenancing, by any thing we have now said, the arrogance of certain preachers and " gifted brethren," who set themselves up as exclusive judges of grace in their neighbours; and, with the most offensive self-sufficiency, go about praying for " unconverted ministers." It would do such men no harm to commune now and then with their own hearts; complying with the advice of Paul to the fastidious teachers at Corinth, who " sought a proof of Christ speaking in him. Examine *yourselves*, whether *ye* be in the faith," lest they fall eventually under the reproof administered to those bloated religionists " which say, *stand by thyself, come not near to me, for I am holier than thou.*"

Piety, however indispensable to the ministry, is not, of itself, an adequate preparation. A man may be a very good man, and yet a very incompetent teacher. The apostle Paul has positively required that he be " apt to teach;"* i. e. have the *faculty* of communicating instruction.

This comprehends

(1.) A *good natural capacity.*

We do not mean that every one who is admitted into the ministry ought to be a man of *genius.* Whatever be suggested by individual vanity, or

---

* Διδακτικος. 1 Tim. iii. 2.

the partial fondness of friends, genius is so extremely rare, that if it were essential to public office, the Christian pulpit, the bench of justice, the university-chair, or the senatorial seat, would very seldom be occupied.—When it does appear, it is misunderstood, fettered, tortured, and, as far as possible, crushed, by vulgar dulness, by scholastic pedants, by that medium race, the mere men of letters—we wish we were not compelled to add—and, too often, by small Theologians. It will, however, force its own way : and as its proper object and work lie out of the ordinary routine of official life, it cannot enter into the standard of fitness for official employment. On genius, therefore, it is vain to insist, for it cannot be had. But a good natural capacity is much more common, and should be peremptorily required. He who is not apt to learn, will never become apt to teach. Most people imagine that education is to do every thing, and nature nothing. But what is the province of education? Not to *create* faculties, but to call them forth. Natural capacity is the material with which education works: It is the soil which she cultivates, and where she sows the seeds of instruction. Expend your utmost labour and skill upon a brick, and you shall never impart to it the polish of marble. Why ? simply for this reason, that it is a brick, and not marble. Let a lad be tolerably stocked with brain, and his improvement in the hands of an *able* preceptor will repay every care, expense, and toil.   But if that important article be wanting, it is a *hiatus valde deflendus*— there is no method of supplying such a lamentable lack.   One would think that this is so evident as to be a mere truism.   And yet, evident as it is, the incessant introduction into the ministry of men whose natural incapacity renders themselves and their office contemptible, shows that it is practically disregarded. We may not dissemble— the interests in jeopardy are too precious to admit of temporizing—It is too notorious to be denied— the very Christian ministry seem determined to try, upon the largest scale, that most absurd and hopeless experiment, the education of a block-head for public usefulness ! The instances, we believe, are comparatively few in which the powers of a youth are put to any reasonable test in order to ascertain whether, in point of intellect, he is really worth training up for the ministry.   College diplomas, considering the dishonourable facility with which they are granted, are but suspicious pledges of either knowledge or talent. Some years ago, a young man who had been originally a maker of brooms, and had " studied divinity," as it is termed, for two or three sessions, was exhibiting a specimen of his improvement before a foreign Presbytery ; and acquitted himself so little to their satisfaction, that they judged it necessary to remand him to his first vocation, as more commensurate with his abilities. This decision was announced by a venerable old minister, in the following manner :—" Young man :. It is the duty of all men to glorify God. But he calls them to glorify him in different ways, according to the gifts he bestows on them. Some he calls to glorify him by preaching the gospel of his Son; and others, by making besoms, (brooms.) Now, it is the unanimous judgment of this Presbytery, that he has not called you to the ministry, since he has not qualified you for it; and, therefore, that it is your duty to go home to your father, and glorify God by decent industry in making besoms."

The mode of the old gentleman was, to be sure, somewhat original; but his spirit ought to pervade the church. Would to God he had dropped his mantle, and that it had been borne on the wings of the wind across the Atlantic. If every preacher incompetent, from a gross defect of natural capacity, were put to the same trade with the young Scotchman, how great would be the increase of brooms !

Some who have accompanied us thus far, will stop short here, and discover a willingness to dispense with acquisitions which were formerly considered as essential to a well-ordered ministry. " Piety," they say, " will keep a man straight upon the main articles of truth ; and strength of mind, though rough and unpolished, will enable him to impart them to others in a plain but impressive manner. This," they will add, "is vastly superiour to the drowsy discourse of hundreds who have been through college, have studied divinity, and pass for great scholars."

We protest, once for all, against learned dulness. Little as we delight in solecisms and uncouthness, we will pardon the maulings of Priscian's* head by the club of untutored power; we shall esteem ourselves repaid for an injury to syntax, or for a rugged illustration, by nature's pathos and vigour; when we should loose our patience with solemn insipidity, or doze under the influences of a leaden diploma; nor deem it any recompense for the loss of our time, that we were put learnedly to sleep. Yet, bad as this is, it is still worse to suffer the insipidity without the poor consolation of some literature to qualify it—an affliction of much more frequent occurrence than the other.

But by what sort of artifice do men cozen their understanding into such argumentation as this? " Talent without education is better than stupidity with it; therefore, talent ought not to be educated ! !" Here is a colt of excellent points and

---

* PRISCIAN, a famous old grammarian. Hence one who violates the rules of grammar, is said to *break Priscian's head.*

mettle ; He is worth a score· of you dull, blundering jades, that have been in harness ever since
they were able to draw ; therefore, he will do very
well without breaking ! It is surprising that so
many, otherwise discreet persons, will maintain
that to be wise and good in the Church of God,
which they know to be absurd and mischievous
in every thing else. In fact, talent, instead of being exempted from the necessity of cultivation, is
alone worth the trouble, and needs cultivation in
proportion to its strength. Talents are born,
knowledge and skill are acquired, God creates the
one ; he has left the other to be obtained by experience and industry. No talent can coin facts ;
and without facts it will run to waste.—Without
information it has no materials to work upon; and
without discipline it will work wrong. The power
of doing evil is in exact proportion to the power
of doing good. Petty minds produce petty harms
and petty benefits. The errours of great minds
are great errours, and draw after them deep, wide,
and lasting consequences. It is of unutterable
moment that they be set right in the beginning.
This, in so far as depends upon human exertion,
is the province of cultivation, which, of course,
makes the

(2.) Part, of " aptness to teach."

What ought it to imbrace in a minister of Jesus
Christ ? We may distribute it into two branches ;

the *first* consisting in literary acquirement; the *second*, in intellectual and moral discipline.

When we consider, that the Scriptures are written in languages which have not been spoken for ages—that they contain a succinct epitome of human history, in reference to the plan of grace, from the beginning to the end of time: going backward to the origin of nations, and forward to their extinction: marking by the sure word of prophecy, the various fates of various people, as well as the principle dispensations of providence toward the Church—that they relate events which cannot be vindicated against plausible objection, without painful research into the phenomena of our globe—that they are full of allusions to the works of God and of man—that they exhibit human character under all its varieties, intellectual and moral; individual and social—that their illustrations of truth, and formulas of speech are borrowed from objects equally strange to our habits and conceptions; from the face of the country; from the soil; from the climate; from the governments; from the idolatry; from the literature; from the state of domestic society; from the manners of the East—that the language of prophecy is wholly peculiar; being a system of symbols, which, though as certain in themselves, and as reducible to fixed laws of interpretation as any alphabetical language whatever, are perfectly un-

intelligible without the study of those laws——
When we consider these things, it is impossible
not to perceive that the study of the Bible allows
of the widest range of learning; and that without
a respectable portion of it no man can "rightly
divide the word of truth."

Acquaintance with the *original tongues* is indispensable.

God has delivered his word to us in Hebrew
and Greek, which being now, as they are commonly called, *dead* languages, are not liable to the
fluctuations of a living one. These are the ulti-
mato and the unalterable standard of truth, by
which every doctrine must eventually be tried.
Excellent versions the Churches have; versions,
from which all that is to make us "wise unto
salvation," may be learned by the humblest pea-
sant or labourer, as certainly as by the accomplished scholar; versions, undoubtedly susceptible
of improvement; but which the licentious spirit
of the times gives us very dubious promise of re-
placing with better. *Timeo Danaos*—we invariably suspect these *amended Bibles*, which the Isca-
riot-bands of professed Christianity are labouring,
on both sides of the Atlantic, to thrust into the
hands of the unlettered and the simple.*

* There is a late most audacious attempt to explain away the
whole gospel of our Lord and Saviour Jesus Christ; absolutely
stripping it, with the single exception of the doctrine of the resur-

But the excellence of versions does not supersede the necessity of studying the originals. The
very fact, that God has preserved them by a care
hardly short of miraculous, would, of itself, establish our position. Why were they committed to
dead languages at all? Why thus carefully preserved amidst the ruined literature of the world,
and the moral midnight of the " dark ages ?" To
be thrown, neglected, into a corner? To be kept
as a curiosity to feed the worms, and amuse the
antiquary? To be decried by gabbling impertinence; or give the ministers of religion an opportunity of displaying their sense and spirit, by
treating as unworthy of *their* study, and as beneath
their notice, those *original* volumes which their
God has not thought it beneath him to consign,
for their use, to the safeguard of his wonder-work-

rection, of every principle which makes it "glad tidings" to a
sinner; substituting in the room of "redemption by the blood of
Christ," a barren morality, little if any better than that of the
Pagans, who were "without Christ, without hope, and without
God in the world;"† and straining into the "cup of salvation" the
distilled venom of Socinian blasphemy. This fatal draught is
handed about with incessant assiduity, and put to the lips of the
unthinking, that they may "sleep the sleep of death." All this under the modest and respectful guise of, " *an improved version of the
New Testament.*" The precedent of such treachery was set long
ago. Its author is "gone to his own place," But the "improved
version," with its accompaniments, show that his treason has not
perished with him. "Betray ye the Son of man with a kiss?"

† Eph. ii. 12.

ing providence ? For ourselves, we doubt not that his chief design in permitting the Hebrew and Greek tongues to die away; in protecting the remnants of classical literature, and causing it to revive, was that his blessed book might be read in the original; and that his Church might be able to assert and maintain his truth inviolate, by having direct access to the fountains themselves. And as little do we doubt that the cry which modern times, and especially modern infidels have raised against classical literature, and in which some Christians and Christian ministers have unwittingly joined, is a deep, though to many an unsuspected stratagem of hell, to bring the original Scriptures into gradual disuse; and, then, by discrediting the versions, to involve Christianity in embarrassment and shame.

Independently on the argument to be derived from the extraordinary preservation of the sacred records, there are other demonstrations of the necessity of studying them in the original.

All human works partake of human infirmity; and are marked with characters of the age in which they are achieved. The remark is universally applicable, because the fact is universally true; and must be so, as it involves a contradiction, or something like one, to suppose it otherwise. The state of the sciences, the style of the fine arts, the very form of handwriting, at a particular period, are stamped with characters by which the date of performances in them can frequently be ascertained, with sufficient precision, many centuries afterwards. If a man write a book which has familiar and frequent references to different subjects of human knowledge, these references must be regulated by the general state of that knowledge; and if it labour under any material defects, must participate in those defects. No enormity of genius, no distance of views and discoveries, like those of Bacon and Newton, beyond the sphere of his contemporaries, will enable him to escape, in *all* things, the common imperfection.

Now the best versions of the Bible are but human works. Stupendous works, indeed, are some of them, all things considered, but still human. They bear strong traces of the state of knowledge upon many subjects at the time when they were made. The effect is, that innumerable passages of Scripture are incorrectly rendered. The vast extension of physical science, of acquaintance with Eastern customs, and even of philology, within the last fifty years, has established a multitude of Scriptural facts; has cleared up a multitude of obscurities; has rectified misrenderings and misinterpretations which no integrity or perspicacity could once avoid; has decisively refuted the objections of enemies. The process is still going on, and will continue to go on. For it is the wonderful property of the book of God, that it has never yet been detected in a mistake, even when speaking on those subjects of which the knowledge was either partially or not at all possessed by the penmen. Its enemies have often charged it with ignorance and errour; but a closer investigation has invariably proved the ignorance and the errour to be their own.

* VOLTAIRE, more malignant than CELSUS, more impudent, if possible, than PAINE, and more witty, peradventure, than all the rest of the goodly brotherhood put together, lost no opportunity of reviling the Scriptures. And if a plump, round lie were now and then necessary to his purpose, as he was not over-nice in his means, he did not permit the want of it to interrupt his " useful labours." Once on a time he made a grand discovery, which was to dock off from the age of the book of Proverbs a handful of centuries, and so prove the book itself to be spurious. He found this good fortune in Chap. xxiii. 31. which the Latin Vulgate renders, " cum splenduerit in *vitro* color ejus," i. e. " when its colour," (wine,) " is brilliant in the *glass*." Now, drinking-glasses, being, according to Mons. Voltaire, a " very recent invention ;" and being mentioned in this text, it follows that the book of Proverbs is *still more recent*, or it could not have mentioned them. Unhappily for the "grand" philosopher, the Hebrew original says nothing about *glass* ; but simply " cup," so that all Mr. V's, argument can prove, at the utmost, is, that the Vulgate translation is later than Solomon ; a most rare discovery ! See the admirable work entitled *Lettres de quelques Juifs a M. de Voltaire.* Tom. III. p. 324, a performance which plays with the flippant infidel even as grimalkin playeth with an unlucky mouse ; and of which the strong sense, superiour learning, grave irony, and blistering wit, threw Voltaire into as

† Dict. Philos. Art. Salomon.

But it is always difficult, and often impracticable, to push our advantages without a knowledge of the original. Under such a privation, the expounder or the advocate of revealed truth must trudge painfully on, yielding a blind credence to the assertion of another; and if, upon any occasion, the fidelity or the competency of his guide should happen to be suspected by himself, or impeached by others, he has no escape from the misery of suspense, or the shame of defeat. But when his acquaintance with the original enables him to measure all criticisms and glosses by that authoritative test, he can take his ground with a promptitude, and keep it with a confidence, second in value only to the ground itself.

Again. All living languages fluctuate. Old words become obsolete; new ones are coined; and of those which remain in vogue, multitudes gradually change their meaning, so as to convey in popular and even classical usage, ideas very different from what they expressed a century before. This fluctuation is extensive and rapid nearly in proportion to the varieties of industry, the competitions of skill, and the intercourse of nations.

---

great a rage, as Beattie's " *Essay on Truth,*" threw the gentle David Hume. The point of their satire remains unblunted, and their reply to Voltaire unanswerable ; notwithstanding the epithet of " *pendant*" applied to their author by Mons. Voltaire's distressed editor, fortified, too, by a philosophic quibble. Vid. *Oeuvres de Voltaire,* Tom. XLIII. p. 131. 8vo. 1785.

Eastern versions of the Bible suffer the least. The Eastern habits and languages being, for obvious reasons, more stable than those of the West. But from the changes which have passed upon the languages of Europe, the vernacular versions, understood according to the present acceptation of their terms, frequently put into the mouth of the sacred writer propositions most foreign to his sense; and lead the unwary reader into false and hurtful conclusions. Strong examples might be adduced from our English Bible; but our limits forbid the detail.

Further. The art of printing has multiplied books, we had almost said, into a nuisance. The multiplication of books has, in its turn, vitiated the art of printing. It has sunk from an employment for talents and erudition, into a mere mechanical craft. The voracious demand for books rendered this unavoidable. United with the boundless circulation of the Scriptures, with the quick succession of editions, and with the low price at which the copies must be furnished for common use, it has increased the number of typographical errours beyond all count. Some of these are of such a nature as to pervert the meaning of the passage, yet to preserve grammar and sense, and to defy correction from the context. Let us mention a curious instance. In 1 Cor. vi. 4. The apostle says, " If ye have judgments of things pertaining to this life, set them to judge who are *least* esteemed in the Church !" One of the editions has it, " set them to judge who are *best* esteemed." A glance at the original detects the mistake. But, setting this aside, no man could tell with certainty, whether we should read " least," or " best;" and a hundred critical arguments might have been mustered to show that the wrong reading is the better.

Besides; there are many things, and those of importance, in every language, which disappear, or rather never appear in a translation. We know that this is doubted, denied, and even laughed at by many. We cannot help it. It is the privilege of ignorance to laugh; of insincerity, to misrepresent; and of captiousness, to doubt. Leaving them in the possession of their several honours, we combine the suffrages of all candid scholars. There is a colouring, a vivacity, a vigour, a comprehension, a pungency of idiom, a felicity of reference in the structure of a word or the peculiarity of a phrase, which never can be transferred. There is a clear opening of sense to an eye practised in the original, which a thick cloud mantles the moment it passes into a version. There is a precision of construction obvious to a scholar of taste, the causes of which are more a matter of feeling than of argument; and though perfectly decisive, are too delicate to be perceived by the uncultivated sense. Yet, in their effects, they tinge and beautify the whole discussion of a subject.

In conclusion. The adversaries of evangelical truth and hope, are much addicted to the practice of assailing our faith through the medium of criticism. What they want in solidity, they make up in boldness and in show. When you press them with the *subject*, they will criticise all your heavy matter away into the thin air of *metaphor ;* little concerned if, in following up their principle, they criticise God himself into a figure of speech. When you press them with a plain text, they will flout at the translation, abuse the translators, and hear nothing but the *original*. When you produce the original, as little to their comfort as the translation, they smell a corruption in the text, and it must be purged by *manuscripts ; any* manuscript being good enough to amend or discard an *ortho-dox* expression. When the manuscripts are rebellious, which commonly happens, unphilosophical Christians as they are, they must receive the castigation of *critical acumen,* i. e. the guesses of an Arian or Socinian mender of the Bible, are to sway our consciences in the question of heaven and eternal life ; or we are to be degraded from the rank of *rational* believers to the pitiable plight of bigots, fanatics, and simpletons.

To repress this effrontery, and to shield the

community from the assaults of this rabid fury; as well as to meet the several exigencies enumerated above, there is no effectual means but the living teacher skilled in the original tongues, and imbued with the correspondent learning. The times awfully demand it. And if such employment does not require a separate profession for the ministry, and able and educated men in it, there is not, and cannot be, a human occupation to which every human being is not always and every where equally competent.

CHURCH OF GOD.

No. X.

Ministry.—Qualifications.

To a critical knowledge of the original tongues, a scribe well instructed in the kingdom of God must add an extensive acquaintance with *facts* necessary for explaining scriptural subjects.

These facts are greatly diversified in their nature, and are to be gathered from various provinces of human research. The more immediately important may be classed under the general heads of *historical* and *physical* facts.

To the historical class belong—

1. Annals; which record distinguished events, ecclesiastical, civil, political, military, commercial, &c.

2. The government, resources, and institutions of a country.

3. The biography of famous individuals.

4. Public and private customs and manners.

5. The state of the sciences, of literature, and of the arts.

The *physical* class comprehends facts relating,

1. To the system of the world—

2. To those phenomena, the study of which forms, what is commonly called, Natural Philosophy; and in which the progress will be short and slow without the help of *mathematics*—

3. To natural geography, geology, &c.

4. To the natural history of animals, especially of man.

The catalogue might easily be enlarged; for there is no department of human knowledge or skill which does not furnish something of value to a good Divine. The design of the foregoing specification is merely to exhibit a summary of things which embrace copious details, and with which an accomplished and well-armed theologian ought to be conversant. An adept in all of them he can hardly become; but such an acquaintance with them as shall enable him to turn their lights in upon obscure parts of the holy writings; and to dissipate the artificial darkness created by the foe, he may and should acquire.

" And can so much human learning—such volumes of history—such long narratives of political things and political men—so much natural philosophy, and astronomy, and geography, and all the rest of it, be necessary to preach the Gospel of salvation? Cannot a minister prove from the Bible that men are lost and perishing, but he must fetch his arguments from the story of kings and kingdoms whereof not one of his audience in twenty ever heard the names? Can he not tell them of Jesus Christ, without telling them of Alexander the Great, or Mahommed, or Genghis Khan? Can he not display the grace of God, without the diagrams of Euclid? nor treat on scriptural symbols, without an algebraical equation? May not his doctrine be heavenly, unless he calculate eclipses? And must he be unable to dig for the hidden treasures of wisdom, without plunging into the belly of a mountain, or the bottom of the sea? Where did the Apostles get such qualifications? What had your human learning to do with the ' mouth and wisdom' with which Peter and John, two *ignorant and unlearned men*, put to silence all the Rabbis of the Sanhedrim? By what means do numbers of the most devoted, faithful, and successful labourers in the Lord's vineyard, make full proof of their ministry, and commend themselves to every man's conscience in the sight of God?"

Against such glowing interrogation, reason wages an unequal war. Confounding and jumbling together things which have no alliance; tacking an absurd conclusion to an acknowledged truth, and pressing the fiction home upon the un-

tutored mind with an air of pious triumph, it cannot fail of persuading multitudes, who fancy they
are convinced because they are amazed; and,
arguing much more from their wonder than from
their understanding, become the intractable converts of zeal without knowledge.

Our reply is short.

The Apostles furnish no precedent. All their
defects were supplied by the inspiration of the
Holy Ghost. What progress would they have
made without it? It will be time enough to quote
them when we are placed in their circumstances,
and can claim their supernatural aids. Let the
Spirit of God be the miraculous instructor, and
we shall immediately dispense with human learning. In that case we will leave the feet of Gama-
liel, and hang upon the lips of a fisherman or a
scavenger. Till then, we hold ourselves excused.
But it is with the worst possible grace that we
are referred to the Apostles as patterns of an *illiterate ministry*, when the Holy Ghost was at the
pains to teach them, *by miracle*, things of which
we are confidently told the Christian ministry have
no need whatever!

As little can be gained by the examples of an
illiterate ministry in later times and among our
selves.

That a plain, uneducated man, of good native
sense, may unfold the elementary, which are the

essential, doctrines of the cross, with propriety, with interest, and with effect—that God has often used, and still uses, the ministry of such men in calling sinners to the fellowship of his Son Jesus Christ, is both true and consolatory. Nay, he has made individuals, alike destitute of information and of talent, the instruments of conversion and confirmation to other individuals of superiour minds and attainments. But we are not, therefore, to pick out all the unlearned lackbrains among Christians, and set them to instruct the men of sense and education. God's sovereignty over-rules our infirmities, our mistakes, and even our follies, for the production of good; when, without his interposition, they could have produced nothing but evil. Yet this does not alter the nature of things. It magnifies, by contrast, the greatness of God; but shows no respect to the littleness of man. Our infirmity is infirmity still; and our follies are follies still. They are not converted into strength, correctness, and wisdom—nor are they to be repeated by us—because God has graciously controlled them for our own benefit and the benefit of others. Talent is his gift; learning is obtained by the favour of his auspicious providence. His people are under a sad delusion when they affect to despise his bounty; and to honour that which it is given to destroy—we mean—*Ignorance.* He is also a sovereign. He may do as it pleaseth him. He can fit his instruments for their work. But his sovereignty is no rule of *our* action; and we must take instruments as we find them; i. e. such as *he* has made them. When we come with *our* offerings, we must bring of our *best*. As we cannot change the nature of means, we are bound to select those, which are, in themselves, best calculated to insure the end. Now ignorance is not so well adapted to instruct as knowledge is: nor can stupidity acquire or apply knowledge as talent can. God employed an ass to rebuke the madness of a prophet; but it does not follow that other asses are destined to a similar office; and are expected to bray as often as they encounter a prophet. We have no objection that modern Balaams shall be put to the same school; but we must first see the same power exerted to qualify the Teacher and *enable* the " dumb ass to speak with man's voice;" or we shall heartily join in requiting the noise of His *Dumbness* with a sound cudgelling; the precedent in the book of Numbers to the contrary notwithstanding.

If good is effected by ignorant imbecility, the true conclusion is, that means make no difference when God chooses to act; as all difficulties are equal, that is, are nothing, to omnipotence. But we abuse our reason; injure the truth; and affront the HOLY ONE, when, from such a fact we conclude, whether formally or practically, that we are to clothe ignorance and imbecility with the authority, and assign them the duties of knowledge and power.   We tacitly put ourselves on a level with God; we indirectly assert our omnipotence. Grant, as we cheerfully do, that, through the divine blessing, good has often been done, and much good too, by persons whom we should have pronounced unfit, on account of either talent or literature, or both, for the ministry of reconciliation —Does it follow, that, with the same blessing upon proper qualifications, the good would not have been much greater; especially as we do not argue on the supposition of miracles? It is a law of God's own enacting, and it is kept in operation by his continual agency, that all bodies shall gravitate, or tend in their motion, toward the center of the earth.   But will a feather, therefore, overcome the resistance of the air as easily, and fall to the ground as rapidly, as a stone, seeing they are both acted upon by the same force? God preserves, by his Spirit, the functions of the animal economy.   Shall, therefore, a kitten draw as much as a horse? It is his visitation which sustains our spirits.   Shall the brains of a fool perform, on this account the intellectual exploits of genius? The analogy is perfect, because the principle is universal, pervading all the divine constitutions with which we have any acquaintance.   The ar-

gument which it furnishes on the point before
us, is irresistible; concluding with the force of
nearly mathematical evidence, against the notion we are combatting; and demonstrating that,
other things being equal, the most intelligent ministry will bring most glory to God, and most happiness to men.   In the mean time, let Christian
ministers and judicatories ponder solemnly the
principle of the following extract from the prophet
Malachi: *Ye brought that which was* TORN, *and the*
LAME, *and the* SICK; *thus ye brought an offering.*
Should I accept this of your hand? saith JEHOVAH.
But CURSED *be the* DECEIVER *which hath in his flock a*
MALE, *and voweth and sacrificeth unto* JEHOVAH *a*
CORRUPT *thing!   For I am a* GREAT KING, *saith the*
LORD *of hosts, and my name is dreadful among the*
heathen.   This fearful commination is levelled
against the PRIESTS *who* PROFANED JEHOVAH'S *name.*
And the profanation consisted precisely in their
consecrating to him the *worse,* when they might
have consecrated the *better.*   " He that hath ears
to hear, let him hear !"

But all such declamation is founded upon a
supposition which is manifestly false : viz. that a
minister of the Gospel has nothing to do in his official instructions, but to insist upon the simplest
doctrines of the Gospel in their simplest form.
That they have been very extensively habituated
to this practice where vital religion is cherished,

admits of no dispute. But that the habit is a good one, admits of much. We institute no comparison between *always* preaching the simple truths of Christ, and not preaching them at all, or preaching them very seldom, and very slightly. When my own conduct is criminated, it is no justification to plead that my neighbour's is worse. The evil to which we object, solemnly and decisively object, is, the keeping Christian people in a state of perpetual childhood. God has charged us to " leave the principles of the doctrines of Christ, and go on to perfection."   He has forbidden us to be continually occupied in " laying the foundation of repentance from dead works; of faith toward God; of the doctrine of baptisms; of laying on of hands; of resurrection of the dead; and of eternal judgment."   Yet it is not to be questioned; the fact is clear as day, that the mass of evangelical ministers never build above the " foundation;" never get out of the principles or mere rudiments of Christianity.   Take what text of the Bible they will, you always find them teaching some one or other of these " rudiments;" always working at some part or other of this foundation.   We do not blame them for this; but for doing nothing else.   For seldom or never rising in their instructions higher than those things which the veriest novices in religion understand almost as well as themselves. There is little consultation of the wants of different classes : little distribution of his portion to every one in due season. There is milk for babes. Good. Let the milk never be withheld : but there should be more. There is no meat for strong men. It is milk, milk, milk. This is the complaint. The effect is, that Christian knowledge is very scanty, and Christian attainments very low: so that hundreds and thousands of our most pious people are ready to be tossed about with every wind of doctrine which does not blow them out the precincts of their elementary principles. There are few incitements to study the Bible. With the exception of some doctrinal passages and moral precepts, it is a book of darkness. Some parts of it are even falling into neglect, and comparative contempt.

Hence the facility with which dissentions multiply, and all manner of sects and pretenders draw away disciples after them. Such is the effect. The immediate cause we have stated. The primary and efficient cause is more remote. *It is in the* DEFECTIVE TRAINING *of the* MINISTRY *itself.* We speak it boldly; because it is a most serious, and a most seasonable, though a painful and unpopular truth. Incapacity we lay aside : but we cannot too deeply lament that where there is not this incurable malady, yet, partly from want of previous preparation, and partly from want of means to pursue their studies after entering upon their functions, the ministers themselves cannot enrich their public instructions. The Bible is not expounded; it cannot be expounded—It is not understood; it cannot be understood by men without learning, however respectable their native powers. Who can illustrate the modes of speech used by the scripture, its allusions, its similes, its parables, its symbols, unimbued with the knowledge of Eastern climate, customs, arts, and institutions? Who can trace and show the accomplishment of prophesy, without large historical inquiry? Who can repel the attacks, and wipe off the aspersions of unbelievers, if he be a stranger to those researches from which the attacks derive their force, and the aspersions their filth? The thing is impossible. In honest truth, the bible is to most of our clergy a sealed book. Their ignorance is unsuspected, because they have, for the most part, to deal with men more ignorant than themselves. But it is not to be conceived how few are the instances in which they could satisfy decent and proper questions, compared with those which should put them to silence. Here is the true secret of that limited sort of preaching which so generally prevails in our pulpits. Our ministry cannot help themselves. They do not know any thing else. Their communications run the length of the *matter* which they have to communicate. Even the fiercest decriers of human learning never forget to display every patch and shred of it which they accidentally pick up. None more sure to turn up the bottom of their treasury than themselves. If any of them chance upon a smattering of letters, his light shall never expire under a bushel : the world shall be in no danger of losing the benefit of his lore. And though in thrusting it out upon his hearers he slander his authorities, by murdering their sense and their names together, he shall be admired as a prodigy, and revered as an Apostle. Say the ministers of religion what they will, if they employ no learning in their ministrations, it is because they have none to employ : and it is adding deception to misfortune, to play off their inability under the mask of a higher degree of spirituality of mind, and a purer desire of glorifying the divine teaching.

The evil is alarming; it is enormous. It has so overgrown our country, and is so deeply rooted, that its eradication by human effort is at best problematical. So long, and so commonly have both ministers and people been accustomed to it, that it is hard to convince many of them of its being an evil at all. The standard of ministerial character has been gradually lowered down from its once imposing elevation to the level of every voluble and boisterous prater. That which was formerly considered as the acquisition " of children and those of weaker capacity," is now, with many, the ministerial attainment.   The Churches have begun to reap the fruits of that tree which their own apathy and parsimony have nourished, if not planted.   The bitter morsel has been only tasted hitherto.   The meal of gall and wormwood is yet to come.   Let them not deceive themselves.   The period of desolation is at hand.   They have been warned and entreated, years and years together, to provide for the suitable education of their ministry; and they have been deaf as adders to the voice of expostulation.   Slow-paced retribution has begun her march, and will fulfil her work. Even now, the United States must be searched through for a single man fit to occupy a post of eminence or of danger ; and the dearth threatens to increase. Let us not have the lullaby of Peace, peace, when fearful facts thicken upon us every hour. If the same apathy shall continue; if strenuous exertions be not speedily, extensively, and perseveringly used, there will be no averting the ruin.   Things must rush on from bad to worse, till the truth of the Gospel is corrupted, its glory obscured, and its power withdrawn, an horrour of thick darkness overspread the land.

" Knowledge is power," in the same sense in which every other instrument may be denominated power ; viz. as a means to an end.   By itself it is as inefficient as any material weapon whatever.   The weapon is useless without a hand to employ it. No better is knowledge detached from a sound head. It would be wasting time to prove that mere learning is among the most feeble and inert of human things. Prodigies of erudition are frequently destitute of common sense; and, in the practical business of life, in all that relates to the direction of men, are more impotent than children. Such reservoirs of unassorted facts answer one good purpose, and only one; they furnish materials for those who can *think.* Heavy plodding industry must be content with the useful property, and the humble praise, of a pioneer for brain. Learning, therefore, although indispensable to an " ability to teach," will not of itself, impart that ability. To give it its proper effect two things are necessary:

1. Good sense.

2. Good sense well disciplined.

On the first we have already expressed our opinion; but its great importance will excuse a few additional remarks.

Were we reduced to the alternative of choosing between good sense without learning, and learning without good sense, we should not hesitate for a moment. Good sense, alone, will be always respectable; learning, alone, almost always ridiculous. No being is so credulous, so easily duped, so regularly absurd, so good for nothing upon an emergency, so utterly incapable of conducting affairs, as a man whose memory is stored with all manner of information, yet is destitute of understanding to use it rightly. Whenever he comes into collision with native vigour, however uncultivated, he is sure to provide the means of his own overthrow. He brings forth his learning with the confidence of victory, and is amazed to find his artillery wrested from him, and turned instantaneously upon himself. Without the sagacity to perceive his error, he is in danger of repeating it as often as he turns disputant. A fact is to him a fact; and the odds are infinitely against him, that out of the million facts at his command, he shall select the one least likely to serve him, and that when, by the misapplication of one part of his learning he has drawn himself into difficulty, he will be unable, with all the rest of it to draw himself out again. The Christian story is full of examples of this mismanagement. Even the pulpit, where the preacher ought at least to be considerate, is doomed to dishonour, when occupied by indiscretion. There are many subjects which *must* be handled, but which require caution, dexterity, and delicacy.

Men of great literature, and even of good manners, who never offend against modesty, make most absurd mistakes in delivering to one audience discourses fit for another of entirely different character. They are very apt to do so, if they have allowed themselves to be absorbed in a particular theme. Their favourite must be the favourite of all the world. Abstruse demonstrations, which years of study have rendered familiar to themselves, must, of course, be evident to the mechanic and the husbandman. An English divine, who was deeply enamoured of the study of *Opticks*, and was a very distinguished proficient in all its minutiæ, could scarcely preach on a text in the bible without sliding into his darling discussions. Accordingly, having to preach to a plain country congregation in Kent, he lectured them with much pith and animation, on his *dioptricks*, and *catoptricks*, his *refractions*, *reflexions*, and *angles of incidence*. They were greatly edified, no doubt; and the preacher was much delighted. It happened, however, that in going from church to the house of a substantial farmer, his host thus accosted him. "*Doctor, you have given us an excellent sermon to-day : but I believe you made one mistake.*" "*Mistake!*" exclaimed the Dr. "*Sir, that is impossible, it was all demonstration ! !*" "*True, your Reverence,*" quoth Hodge, "*but them there things that you preached so much about you called Hop*STICKS; *now in our country, here in Kent, we call 'em Hop-*POLES." We think we have heard, in the course of our lives, sermons nearly as well adapted to time and place, and quite as instructive to the people.

The injudicious treatment of types, parables,

and all figurative language, has been so common,
that it ceases to surprise and almost to displease.
Habit gradually renders us insensible to faults
which, at first, strike us with great force; and the
unquestioned piety of many public teachers serves
as a mantle for even their absurdity. In every
walk of life, superiors will be imitated by inferiors.
Blemishes are much more easily copied than excellence; and when the aberrations of thought
have imparted respectability to a bad taste, the
evil becomes almost incurable in minds of a secondary order. The irregular sportings of an
active and untrained imagination, seduce, by their
glare, the footsteps of imitation; and, what was,
in the original, a splendid defect, becomes in the
copy an unpardonable offence. Thus have successive generations of preachers regularly improv-
ing upon bad models, displayed their ingenuity in
marring the beauty of the Scripture, in destroying
the harmony of its parts, in breaking off the fine
points of its most exquisite passages; and when
they have committed all these ravages, and converted the book of God into a book of quibbles
and conundrums, they please themselves with the
self-flattery of having performed wonders of instruction and edification. Typical and figurative
texts must be hunted to death. The more points
of resemblance, the abler, of course, is the preacher; and the more he can find in a figure than

other people can, the more, are they taught to believe, do they see of the fulness of the Scriptures. *How* he made his discoveries, is a question which few think of asking. The marvellous has a patent for a sort of implicit faith. For the many, it is sufficient that he made them; sagaciously concluding that if the wonders had not been there, he could not have found them. There is, indeed, one consolation, and it is not a small one, that preachers who love the precious doctrines of the cross, will preach what is true in itself, however they may desert or mangle their texts. Yet this is no excuse for coupling with it all manner of nonsense, and fathering it upon the wisdom of God.

The most insufferable departure from the principles of sound exposition is that perversion of the plain facts of the Bible which is called *spiritualizing them.* As if there were not passages enough which contain fairly and unequivocally, according to the laws of proper construction, every doctrine of the Gospel! as if the Spirit of God had not made his own book spiritual enough!

It is inconceivable what havoc this species of mania, for it deserves no better name, has made in the sober and dignified lessons of divine revelation. And it shows how powerful is the influence of an irrational fashion, when even great men are swept by it into the bog of absurdity. Massillon's sermon on the impotent folk around the pool of Bethesda, with all its eloquence, cannot escape from this censure. We have before us a thing called a sermon, prepared for the press too; which is a *morceau* in this kind of skill.

The author takes for his subject the history of Ehud's adventure when he killed Eglon, the king of Moab, and delivered Israel. After pathetically lamenting, in his introduction, the blindness of those who perceive in the context nothing but a plain history, he proceeds to unfold the mysteries which unveiled themselves to his eye. Every thing is transformed into a type. Ehud is a type; his dagger is a type; his left-handedness a type; the quarries by which he passed a type. In a word, he and his adventure are types of Christ and his providence. Eglon, too, is a type; a type of Satan; his big belly, fat, dirt, and all. But how was Eglon's *fat* typical of Satan? You may wonder, reader, but if you have any sense, you will never guess——Why even thus. Satan is the god of this world; he works in the children of disobedience. These children of disobedience are a vast multitude. The whole of them together serve as a *body* for Satan; so that he is a *fat* devil indeed! We are not caricaturing. We are relating a simple fact without exaggeration, and even *below* the truth! And this vile gibberish must be palmed upon plain people as *spiritual* preaching! Another sample occurred in a discourse upon Gen. xxix. 2. where Jacob is related to have " looked, and behold, a well in the field ; and lo ! there were three flocks of sheep lying by it." This is all type.— The three flocks typify the three dispensations, to wit, the Patriarchal, the Mosaic, and the Christian. The well, too, is typical. And the preacher having desired his hearers carefully to observe that the " well was in the field," broke out into this edifying exclamation, " What a mercy, my brethren, that the *field was not in the well ! !*"

We have quoted strong cases, but not stronger than others we could quote. They are the genuine consequences of that vicious mode of parodying the Bible, from which good sense is the only preservative. Considering how much of this harlequin trumpery is bandied about in the Church under the garb of *spiritual preaching*, it is little short of a miracle that the religion of Christ Jesus is not burlesqued out of the world.*

---

* This number was never finished by the author. Nor has any paper been found, containing his thoughts upon "the mode of preserving, a standing ministry," which was to form the last topic of this series.—ED.